Before I AM

The Direct Recognition of our Original Self

ॐ

Before I AM

The Direct Recognition of our Original Self

Dialogues with Mooji

Book I

Edited and Designed by
Sharon Hogan
Andreana Fay
Nataraaj (Noé J. Peyre)

arunachala press

ARUNACHALA PRESS

An imprint of STONE HILL FOUNDATION PUBLISHING

37/3352 Palliparambu Lane, Cochin 682017, Kerala, India

arunachalapress@asianetindia.com

stonehillfoundation@asianetindia.com

Before I Am: The Direct Recognition of Our Original Self
Copyright © 2008, 2009, 2010 by Mooji. All rights reserved.
First edition published 2008 in India as an Arunachala Press
original paperback
Reprinted 2009, 2010
ISBN 10: 81-89658-18-2
ISBN 13: 978-81-89658-18-2
A South Asian edition of this book has been published under the
Editions India imprint. Reprinted 2009, 2010.

Book Editing and Design:
  Sharon Hogan, Andreana Fay, Nataraaj (Noé Peyre)
Cover Design:
  Nataraaj (Noé Peyre), Vistar Simone Ferraresi
Photography on cover and on pages 71, 72 (bottom photo) and 149:
  Monica Onore

Book composition by BookWorks STM, Cochin
Printed in India by The Ind-Com Press, Chennai
Printed on acid-free, partially recycled paper
Distributed in South Asia by Stone Hill Foundation Media

This is not a book
to please your mind.

It is a book
to dethrone your mind
and set your Heart free.

Bhagavan Sri Ramana Maharshi
The Sage of Arunachala
Guru of Sri Poonja

*"Mind extinct, the mighty seer
returns to his own natural being
and has no action to perform."*

Sri Harilal Poonja
Beloved 'Papaji'

Prostrations at the feet of my Master

the embodiment of grace, wisdom and love;
the light of whose presence
dispels all doubts and delusion,
thus establishing the mind in its original state
– unborn awareness.

You have looked all over the world,
but unless you see your Self first
you will never see anything else.
First look at who you are
and then, if need be,
look at anything else in the world.

If you see your Self
you don't even have to look to God.

~ Papaji

Contents

For a moment, don't fix anything I'm saying here.
Don't make tattoos out of any utterance.

Just stay open, quiet and alert
and the unfolding work of Grace
will be recognised and felt,
within and without,
as harmony and love

in service to itself.

'The second thorn'

In India, there is a saying: "If a thorn goes into your foot, you might use a second thorn to remove the first thorn. And then you throw both thorns away."

This book is effectively a second thorn. Its purpose is to remove the thorns of conditioning and habit which are picked up in the forest of existence, and which appear to hinder or make painful what could be a joy-filled dance. Its intention is to point to the essential truth of who and what we are: the unchanging, pristine Awareness in which the play of the manifest world appears. Mooji's words can therefore be considered the second thorn which removes all thorns, pointing, as they do, to the living truth that is our own being. Their aim is that we recognise there is no need to search for this truth outside ourselves, for it is our innermost reality. When what this book is pointing to is truly assimilated, then we're finished! It has returned us to where we have always been.

The content of this book comes from live recordings, dialogues, Skype meetings and one-to-one or private interviews, which took place between Mooji and seekers who came to meet with him in England, Ireland, Italy and India from 2004 to 2006. Many requests were made to have copies of some of these conversations, and in response to this, recordings of the talks began. The book you now hold in your hands came out of these recordings, lovingly transcribed, edited and presented by Mooji and friends who wish to share the joy of 'Satsang', as these dialogues are called. Some parts of the dialogues have been edited in order to further clarify or lay greater emphasis on the truth which Mooji lives to share.

Read these pages as systematically, as sporadically, or as spontaneously, as suits your mood in the moment — each, any and every page may speak to you, because truth requires no method, cannot be categorised and is not chronological. Anywhere you open this book and meet these words, these words will meet you.

Any moment is a moment for stepping into the fire. This fire will not burn you, it will only burn what you are not. When you are touched by grace — and don't doubt it, grace is already operating right here by even placing this book in your hands — surrender to it. Don't try to understand or solve the mystery; be willing instead to be dissolved into the mystery itself.

You are being introduced to you without you, through the medium of these words — Self recognising Self through the mirror of inquiry. Nothing else needs to happen. In any case, "Nothing ever happened", as Mooji's Master, Papaji, declares. The job, if there was ever such a thing, is done.

To change the world is not your mission.

To change yourself is not your duty.

To awaken to your true nature is your opportunity.

A first encounter with Mooji

I first met Mooji in Brixton Market, London, in February, 1999. At that time he was selling incense in the market and I was working at the French Embassy. Shortly afterwards, we met in his small flat for tea and had our first conversation. We ended up talking all through the night. Time vanished! I was amazed. As the talk deepened, I couldn't believe what I was hearing and what I had in front of me. I had discovered someone of the like of Socrates or an Indian sage of yore under the guise of a friendly and unassuming form. The deepest wisdom was pouring from his lips as I eagerly expressed all the questions which had been burning inside me for years, and I was finding at last living, direct — and baffling! — responses to them. These were not merely intellectual answers but rather a direct and authoritative pointing towards something which is altogether beyond the realm of understanding. For years, I'd been reading philosophical and spiritual books, but now I was face-to-face with the living embodiment of the Truth I'd been reading about, right in front of me. Right away, Mooji made clear to me my own deep nature: this awareness, this emptiness, which nothing can improve or impair.

Since then, I have had many occasions to witness his wisdom in action, wonderfully suited to the minds of those who come to him, a wisdom which springs smoothly from the uninterrupted source of living experience. It springs from, and is felt as, Love — tremendous, genuine and pure.

Nataraaj (Noé J. Peyre)

Mooji selling incense
Brixton market, London, circa 1996

*Self-inquiry brings the mind back
to ground zero,
to the bare 'I am'.*

*Witnessing of this 'I am'
occurs in the Absolute.*

Recognising the Self

Mooji, could you explain Self-inquiry? How do I actually begin?

Begin thus: 'I am' – This is the most natural recognition and knowledge. The sense of existence is spontaneously felt in you as 'I am'. No-one taught this to you. Be aware of this simple intuition without associating it with other thoughts. Feel how it is to be simply present, in this instant, without holding onto any intention. Don't touch any thought of doing something special. Keep inwardly quiet. If suddenly, a wave of thoughts should come, don't panic. There is no need to control or suppress them. Simply, let them play without your involvement. Observe with detachment. Remain empty of intention. Keep quiet.

Imagine you are standing on a platform at the railway station. One by one the trains come: they stop, doors open, doors close, they move on. You don't have to get on. Like this, simply observe the thought-activity appearing on the screen of consciousness without connecting up. Don't log on. Thoughts and sensations will be seen to move on by themselves, without being forced. Stay neutral. Be with the awareness as awareness itself. Feel the breath moving effortlessly, without will or strain. Observe the senses functioning, the sense of outer and inner, any movement, just 'happening' by itself, unplanned and unforced.

Whatever arises as thought, feeling, movement or sensation is quietly observed, only now there is less interest, less pull. All is arising; your self is not aroused. All this is smoothly observed. Now, even the sense of self – the feeling 'I am' – is inside this awareness. Make no greater effort than is required. You are here. That which is neither doing nor undoing, neither directing activity nor being affected by activity, which is effortlessly aware yet unconcerned: That, is your real Self. Not behind nor in front, nor above nor beneath – for it is not another phenomenon. It is unplaced, unborn, boundless Self.

Now, observe the observer: 'Who am I?' Check inwardly but remain quiet with alert attention. Don't collect any answer or clues; an answer would and could only be an opinion, an idea of another concept. Don't tie yourself to any concept. Turn the attention away from objects and toward the viewing subject. What and where is the seer? Remain silent and neutral. There should now be an increased strength of focus in the looking.

Now, again, watch the sense 'I am'. What is 'I'? From where does it arise? Watch. What do you find?

It cannot be found. It does not exist.

It cannot be found objectively. Nevertheless, the 'I'-sense or intuition continues to be present. It is the non-finding of 'I', phenomenally, that proves its non-objective existence. 'I' or 'I am' is found to be without form, an intuition arising from, in, and as, emptiness. Without focused inquiry, 'I' appears to be an entity comprising body and conditioned mind. When searched for as a form, it is found to be merely a thought; the form of 'I' is thought. Formless, it arises from emptiness as the intuitive sense of subjective 'presence'.

Now that 'I' is found to be formless presence, what recognises this? Does this possess form?

Inquire like this.

Thank you, Mooji.

You are most welcome.

Whatever direction you take,
the needle of the compass always points north.

So it should be with you.

Whatever you do or wherever you go,
let your mind remain
in your heart.

What am I?

Who or what am I really?

Don't touch the 'I' and you will know.

... And now?

There's agitation and an attempt to go behind that.

What is trying to go behind that? Drop this idea of going behind. Stay where you are. So agitation is felt, what is getting agitated, disturbed?

My mind.

What watches agitated mind? Is *that* agitated?

No ...

That in which mind and its content is seen, can that itself be seen? Can it be described, touched or caught?

No. It has no quality.

And you who knows this: where are you in this? What are you?

I am not separate. I cannot say or describe what I find. When I try to speak about it, words carry me away into mind again.

5

Actually, that is not true. It is a popular myth and creates much mischief when believed. In truth, nothing takes you away from what you are. It is your attention which goes out. You watch the movement of attention; therefore, you remain behind. Look deeply into this and both yourself and this idea of leaving yourself will fall away. What watches leaving and returning?

That cannot be known. It is quality-less.

You are right in saying it cannot be known. You can only *be* that. Then there is no separation in knowing and being. Is there something you must do to remain here? Is there a 'you' as a tangible entity who is capable of leaving or returning?

Beneath the ever-flowing stream of sensations including mind and the 'I'-sense, there is only this. The wise refer to it as the sole reality – as 'That which is.' It could also be referred to as: *'Buddha-being but no Buddha.'*

[*Silence*]

... Now, what inquiry is needed? Inquiry is necessary only when the sense 'I' arises and swells up with identification to the extent that detached and silent observation seems eclipsed or overpowered by intense personal identification with the unreal. Should this occur, find out immediately who is affected or involved in that play. Who suffers? Keep quiet, dive within and track down 'the sufferer'. Is it real? Tangible? Can it be held in view?

Watch, as this question bites in, the tendency to lapse into sleepiness, or the attention suddenly veering off towards some trivial pursuit. These are common psyche reactions. This is a form of avoidance from the ego. It is as if it throws a stone in the bush in order to put you off its scent and so avoid detection. Hold to the task and don't abandon the inquiry! Focus the attention on locating the one who is suffering. Like this, it is found that no-one is there to suffer. It is the idea I have of myself that apparently suffers. What discovers this? Again, it is found that there is simply discovering but no individual discoverer.

It is not enough that you believe these words being said — this, you must discover by experiencing it for yourself. Only then does the grip of the ego's influence loosen and is the spell of delusion broken. The one Self alone shines inside the body as 'I am.' In each body it is reflected like one facet of an infinitely-faceted diamond with each facet having the total diamond behind it. This effortless knowledge is revealed in one who has discovered through self-inquiry or surrender, the unreality of the ego-mind.

How can I speak or act from this No-one-ness, Mooji?

Just rest with this question, be quiet with it, and see what is there to be discovered. Truly, That Which Is neither speaks nor acts. It is beyond action and activity. This is at the very pinnacle of ultimate understanding. What or who am I? Can what I am be seen? And by

7

whom? Am I two? Can I find myself? Are there two entities acting as a single I? If so, which is real? And how to know? Am I split as half and half?

These questions cannot be answered by the mind with any lasting satisfaction. Such questions asked within the light of inquiry are deeply penetrative, introspective and explosive scout-questions. Sometimes they explode, other times – they implode! When asked with focused attention and urge they are bound to stir up some deep response inside our being. I call the question 'Who am I?' my piranha question – it devours the questioner! Something goes off inside, and whatever goes off inside is out of your hands; it's no more your business! Like the food you're chewing, that's your business, you enjoy it; but once it is swallowed, it's gone, out of reach. Something else takes over now. I call it Grace.

Can there not be awakening without grace? What is the work of grace?

Grace is essential for liberation. It is synonymous with freedom. Grace is the activity of the Sat Guru – our inmost reality. Grace is divine benevolence pampering itself.

Forget the answer and dive into the question

What do you mean when you speak of liberation, Mooji?

Liberation is the natural outcome of sincere and steady investigation into the nature of self. One sees that all that arises as manifestation, including the personality, is a play of consciousness in the fullness of the Absolute. In the recognition of this timeless fact, unbroken joy and peace shine inside the heart, body and mind. This is the real power of inquiry: to reveal the Awareness Self as the source of all appearances.

But who is inquiring?

Forget about the answer and dive deep into the question. All answers come from the mind. 'I' must be there to say "I am pleased or displeased by this answer." What is 'I'? Find out what the 'I' is and you will find who inquires.

There is no 'I.'

What is saying this?

It is arising in consciousness spontaneously.

And you, who are you? What notices this or anything? If you truly look and pay attention to your own findings, I will stop asking these questions. If you want me to stop hammering at your mind, look and resolve this dilemma for yourself.

I'm that something. Whatever it is …

Prior to the arising of the statement 'I am that something,' what is here?

[*Silence*]

… Whenever I am into the inquiry, I reach a point where no answer comes …

What observes this?

Consciousness … Emptiness? … Something …

Stop throwing peanuts at me. These are empty words, someone else's words and testament, not your own. Can't you feel that they lack authority and conviction? Speak from your own direct experience alone. Look within. No thinking, imagining or visualising is required, only focused observation is of value here. This power is already in you. Whatever arises is observable and is therefore watched from somewhere beyond. What is it that stands apart and watches? Does it possess quality? Is it a something?

No, it isn't a something …

What knows this? From where are you observing, at this very point, give some feedback if you can – what is happening now?

Umm … there's … something that is seen by nothing … and I am before that.

BE That!

[*Silence*]

Can you come out of this?

No … I cannot. What I am, cannot … what I really am, is always here.

[*Silence*]

I came here to share with you this good news: You are complete. You are perfection, beyond the concept of perfection. You are the eternal principle – you are there before the concept 'I am' arose, immovable. From the highest standpoint, you perceive everything as your play. You are all there is.

Discover and confirm this for yourself. It must become your own experience. Don't quote from what you have read or heard. Read from your own book, the book of your Self, this unshakeable truth.

*Whatever your attention grasps
becomes your experience.*

*You are aware
of that experience.*

What knows both experience and experience-er?

Find that.

Be that.

Stay as the formless

This morning I called you because I was scared. There was only emptiness, 'Mary' [questioner's name] couldn't be found ... I was not there! It was really scary!

All is well. You were there but not personally, otherwise, what would witness emptiness? You were tasting the fruits of your own inquiry. The sense that something, your old idea of self, is vanishing: this was being witnessed. Fear arises as the old reference points are eroding away, but this is also witnessed. What was there, witnessing all of this? All searching is ultimately for one thing only: to find the seeker. What is it that is searching? Can the seeker be found? Is the seeker a tangible, measurable entity?

What exactly is it that I am then?

No one else's answer will do. It is said only the *sattvic* mind can ask this question. *Sattvic* mind means the pure mind which is free from distractions and searches for one thing only – ultimate liberation. That mind is the divine mind itself. The wise say: only that life is truly auspicious in which the question 'Who am I?' arises and is recognised and pursued until one is free from the bewitching influence of the mind.

I can say I've seen that I'm not the mind and that my personality is an idea, but there is also a thought that somehow it could become more clear, that more could be done.

Let's look closely at this 'I' that you perceive yourself to be, the one that thinks it could do more, or feels itself getting closer to some goal. Today, in this instant, I want you to recognise that you are not different from Buddha, that you are Buddha itself, that you are the same consciousness as Christ's consciousness. You are not fully aware of this because you have adopted and identified the body and mind not only as your expression but also as your real being, therefore you perceive yourself to be changeful as body and mind are. As long as you cling to the idea of being a personal entity, you will imagine you have some task to 'stay' as the self – which you cannot do, no one can. You become very frustrated with the sense of being limited. Even 'realisation,' you will feel as a passing experience because your 'I' is rooted in separation itself.

There is the 'I' which arises with historical and psychological force. It is associated with various qualities and tendencies. It comes from mind, and is mind itself. There is also the 'I' which arises from boundless space and is without form. Discern which is real. The personal 'I' is full of quality and self-seeking. Its self-consciousness is rooted in identity with the body and is therefore easily detectable as a phenomenon. That which witnesses this personal 'I-me' and its limitations may also be felt as 'I', but is more subtle, formless. This is the 'I-Self', shining within the body as space, silence, intuitive knowing and bliss. Beyond 'I-me-ness' is the ever-perfect reality-awareness Self.

[*Silence*]

So ... as long as my attention is going to what arises, as long as there is an object perceived by a subject, there will always be duality. Therefore, at some point I must drop even the search itself, no?

In truth, you don't drop anything. What actually happens is that at an auspicious moment, the search drops you! It is you that is dropped! Sri Ramana said: "Keep on inquiring until there is nobody left to inquire." I describe this surrender as like watching a meteorite, a shooting star that disintegrates as it enters the earth's atmosphere. As you continue inquiring, the inquirer fades away.

There was once a great *yogini* who meditated deeply on the following: 'I am here. I can clearly feel my being, so what exactly perceives even this beingness?' As her consciousness deepened into a state of intense focus, there was a sudden awareness of the most beautiful sounds, such as she had never heard before. "Oh, how delightful!" she thought, "but they cannot be what I am, because I am here to hear them!" Some moments passed, and then there appeared a blaze of fantastic colours shimmering with brilliance. But again came the recognition: "How beautiful, how sensuous! But they have nothing to do with what I am, because I'm

15

here, unaffected, perceiving them. Even that which is captivated by their beauty is perceived in my Self." After another short while, celestial Beings began appearing, floating in space and glowing with light and love. And again came the discernment: "Oh, how wonderful a vision! But I cannot be whatever they are, for I'm already here experiencing their appearance!" Finally, all the various phenomena merged into an all-encompassing silence, beyond duality.

Even this emptiness of which you spoke earlier, even this cannot be what you are, since it is perceived phenomenally. Therefore, I say you are emptiness beyond even the concept of emptiness. And when ultimate understanding happens, even this realisation is 'watched', as it were, in what Is. Everything goes back into silence, and there's nobody there to assess the silence. Silence is not disturbed by thought or speech. Space is not affected by whatever appears in it. You are that. Stay in this image-less seeing.

Om.

To die before I die

I'm trying to find the right words, Mooji, to find my clearest question for you ...

I say: shoot the questioner! [*Laughter*]

You know, there is something commanding about that question which springs directly from the heart. It does not have to be styled in some philosophical language or posture. It can be the most simple thing, yet there's great power in its freshness and innocence and so the beingness rushes forth to satisfy its call. Yes, like a yearning, like the stretched-out arms of a crying child, something within rushes out to meet it and to absorb it into itself. The mind rarely asks from this place. Questions coming from mind rarely come with this bite, this urge, this innocence.

Some time ago, a man came to satsang and asked, "Can I see you privately?" I said okay, come. When he arrived, I asked him, "Why did you ask for a one-to-one?" He said: "It is a matter of some urgency for me. The doctors have told me I have a terminal condition, they said that I am dying. And I have come to see you because I want to die before I die."

Who else comes with this urgency, this plea: "I want to die before I die?"

[*Long silence*]

... Mooji, I'm not exactly sure what he meant ...

He meant: I want to stop being molested by the ego. I want to stop it determining the quality of my existence, before it naturally falls down by itself. I want to be free of the influence of the ego. I wish for an end to this hypnotic state of believing that I am this person who is going to die. Somewhere deep inside there is a recognition that what has been believed until now is not true. There is great sense of inadequacy in the conception of myself as merely my body/mind functioning. There is a claustrophobia somewhere in me and my beingness longs to breathe without being harassed by these thoughts. This is what I perceive he meant.

... How could he achieve all that?

By finding out who or what his Self is.

One must be clear about the real position. Once it is irrefutably clear that I am that in which witnessing of the world takes place, that I am not that which is perceived, that I am beyond all forms and modifications, the effect of the seeing will follow spontaneously, perhaps even unconsciously.

I remember Papaji telling me: "If you wish to be one with the truth, *you* must vanish, *you* must disappear!" Up until that point, there had been years of bliss and joy. There had been a sense of being immensely blessed, chosen as a servant of God even. Suddenly, in the presence of the master, in the hearing of these words, a great storm arose within my heart. Fierce resistance, anger and judgement flared up. My mind wanted to escape this throat-cutter, so it pictured him as a charlatan. "I cannot surrender to you. Now, if Ramana was here – ahhhhh ... He, I know, is the real thing." But you see, Papaji wasn't instructing my ego to do something special like 'vanish', he merely spoke from truth, and the force emanating from there exposed the ego, grabbing it by the throat – it came up kicking and screaming. All, *all*, was the Master's grace. The offender was exposed and blasted, and there followed immense peace, unbound silence and a new love, a very powerful love towards the Master.

I remember that before my *execution*, some resistance was always in my mind. Sometimes Papaji would say some frivolous, inaccurate thing and I would feel my mind judging: "Papaji, that's not true. If you were a true Master, you wouldn't say this or that thing." I kept up this judgement to protect my ego for as long as I could but somehow inevitably came to feel the cool blade of the Master's sword moving ever closer, moment by moment. Ego always has an escape plan, a back door.

I don't know why I am telling you all this. Maybe I just want you to realise that you cannot design the way in which your mind will vanish. Something pulls you there, to the butcher's block. The Beingness has brought itself in the form of mind to be reminded, to rediscover, that it is object-less awareness – no thing, everything, and beyond.

Sri Nisargadatta Maharaj expressed this beautifully: "When I see that I am nothing," he said, "this is Wisdom. And when I see that I am everything – this is Love. And, between these two valleys, my life is flowing." Sometimes you will see, like now and here with me, that you are nothing tangible, objective or knowable. You will also discover there's no-one personally seeking or discovering. The 'seeking' is like an impulse from the Self to rediscover itself. There is just this expanse of Being; a subtle intuition; and inside this, a wave of great love flows without interruption.

Be bold and fire your bodyguards, for they cheat you out of real freedom while appearing to be your protectors. Take your door off the hinges. Pull down your walls. Allow yourself to be completely undressed by grace so that you may begin seeing with the eyes of God.

You are the eternal being, beyond becoming. Witnessing, but not a witness-er. Let all come and go.

One day this body, too, will go. You will witness that also.

[*Long silence*]

But you are that which remains unaltered by all that comes and goes.

Mooji, I can feel the truth of this when I hear you speak of it, but when I leave here, when I'm back in the world, I seem unable to really remember this feeling ...

If I tell you a hundred times that you are one hundred percent truth always, that you are one hundred percent free, that you are the one eternal principle, that your nature is joy, freedom and peace, you will be delighted to hear it a hundred times, and a hundred times you will forget it. Why? Because for thousands of times, you have embraced the idea that you are *not* free, not yet, that you're not ready, not worthy, that more needs to be done. You have put so much effort into transforming a shadow into an object it is only a reflection of!

[*Silence*]

Your body was born but *you* were never born. *You* shall never die. Discover this now, while you have the body! Body will pass. I say, find that which cannot pass. This opportunity is available now – take hold of it. Find out: who says "I" inside this body? Does it have an age, a size? A design? Find this out with full devotion and attention.

Now is the auspicious moment.

21

Enjoy life's pleasures,
but don't forget what you are.
Like this, nothing binds you.

Then, when Life bites,
accept this also as a friend, a gift.

This bite tells you:

Don't attach yourself to me.
I, too, am here to remind you
that all this is unreal.

Suffering your experiencing

What about physical pain? What about suffering?

Hand over your existence to existence and keep quiet.
All is Grace.

If you really had the free will and power to shape
your destiny, create your ideal life, you would, most
probably, leave out all discomforts, all that challenges
your ego, all that exposes feelings of guilt or shame or
anything that threatens your attachments. You would
exclude all these and replace them with chocolate-
flavoured moments. [*Laughter*] But however much you
endeavoured to construct and secure a life that satisfied
your projection, you would still fail to match, in quality and auspiciousness, the life that is unfolding without
human intention.

A man once said to Sri Nisargadatta: "Maharaj, your
words resonate deep within my heart. I feel their
power and know them to be true. But if I am to be
honest in describing my experience, I would have to
admit that throughout my life, I'm continuously experiencing suffering!" And Maharaj replied: "No, this is
not true. You are not experiencing suffering; you are
suffering your experiencing."

Can you say more about Nisargadatta's words, Mooji?

I will tell you a story.

In great pain, a man went to see the doctor. "How can I help you?" the doctor asked him. "I hurt all over, doctor," said the man. "Whenever I touch here," he explained, touching a spot near his heart with his finger, "it hurts! And if I touch here," he added, touching his nose, "ouch! – it also hurts!" The doctor looked on, perplexed, as the man continued. "When I touch here," he said, touching his stomach, "it hurts like hell!" Then he leaned towards the doctor and touched his eyelid with his finger. "Ooouch!" he yelled again. So, the doctor conducted a complete physical examination on the man. Finally, "Sir," the doctor said, "I can find nothing wrong with the areas you showed me. The trouble is, you have a broken finger!" [*Laughter*]

'I' is this finger. Wherever 'I' goes, there is always trouble. This 'I' is ego: "I like, I dislike." Whatever it touches, in ignorance, causes itself and others pain. Yet it imagines pain is caused by 'other'. When, through grace, it is realised that 'I-ego' is the cause of suffering, and that 'I-ego' is dreamed in being, suffering ends.

Identification with this 'I' is at the root of suffering. When you choose what you should experience – you suffer. When you choose who you should learn from – you suffer. When you are constantly interpreting how things are or how they should be, what you deserve and what you do not deserve – you suffer. Wherever there is pride, attachments, judgements and desires, there is suffering. When we awaken from ignorance into our true nature – suffering is absent.

But Mooji, how can you not feel it if there's strong physical pain?

Pain and pleasure both belong to the body. It's a package deal. Once you take a body, you'll experience all the interrelated opposites and contrasts of the dance we call life.

But this does not mean you suffer automatically because the body is there. Identity amplifies suffering. In impartial and impersonal observation of the body/mind functioning, pain is perceived as natural phenomenon. Non-personal experiencing is itself freedom. Nevertheless, for some people, suffering seems to be an inescapable aspect of the human experience. In the realm of sentient experience, suffering is unavoidable. Where there is strong psychological and physical identity, there is proportionate suffering – it's the tax for having a life!

So, you say: "I've suffered." I'm not going to fight with you about it. But also there are people who are suffering with a deep sense of gratitude or even joy behind their apparent suffering. I won't call this suffering really, because there is no resistance here. They've understood and accepted that grace sometimes manifests as an intense inner burning that purges the being of conceptual and emotional toxins, and to that extent they remain in peace.

I don't know how I'd feel grateful when pain, physical or emotional, is really throbbing!

There is no need to force being grateful. Due to a kind of conditioned reflex, the blood-flow rushes towards the centre of activity like the flow of white corpuscles to the site of physical injury. In this example, the centre of activity is wherever the sense of personal 'I' throbs, and the subsequent attention given to it is like the blood flow.

You are not that: you are *aware* of that. Just be clear about this, without panic. If you hold to the intuition, the sense 'I am,' and don't allow this to connect with any other concept, if you just let the 'I am' incubate in itself – immediately, joy and space prevails. Spontaneously, there is the silent and intuitive conviction: "I am timeless, unbound being." This is not a teaching – it's a powerful, inner experience – inexplicable. Thankfully, you don't have to write a thesis about it. Something is seen, it's enough. You cannot prove it and you needn't prove it. You don't need to talk about it, nor even to share it. Keep quiet.

Remain in that natural inner solitude.

[*Long silence*]

The land of 'I don't know'

In the Inquiry, one is not to get involved in what is arising. One is just witnessing, just listening, just looking at it, is that it? Well, what's the difference between emotionally feeling, and listening to the Being? There seems to be a kind of tuning in ...

Even 'listening to the being' is too much. Just be. *Be* being. You are already that.

If you think "I must listen to the being," you create some sort of split, a separation, and now there is a task to re-unite one thing with another. This is the birth of duality. Instantly, a 'me' is created who must listen to the Self. This is a very subtle trap, and most believe it. Who is it who will listen to the being? You *are* the being! These are all mischievous thoughts; detect them and reject them swiftly.

It's just that sometimes I get confused between listening to emotions that arise, and thinking of all that arises as just contractions in the Beingness. And then there's a remembering that it's all just mind-stuff anyway! But then I ...

All these concepts have become very heavy, very burdensome. Put them down. If you pick them up, they will weigh you down and give you strenuous and value-less tasks to accomplish. Your mind lacks power and clarity because your attention has split away from the source and is flapping about. Don't split off into the veins, stay in the main artery. What does this mean? It means remain as the witnessing core only. Don't involve yourself with what comes and goes. What do you require to simply be? Something?

No, not really ...

But maybe secretly you entertain some fantasy about being someone special. Maybe you want to levitate in front of your friends or something! [*Laughter*] Or perhaps it's that you wish, let's say, for the power to heal people, or to predict the future. Should any of these accomplishments come to you, I tell you that these will become mere distractions for the ego. If you hanker after such special effects, you will not know true freedom. Give up all aspirations and intentions and keep quiet, and then see if you lack anything when you remain without desire and association. Just be still. Touch nothing.

You say that all the time ...

Yes, but do you *listen?* [*Laughter*] And do you apply that advice? Perhaps, that is why I say it all the time! [*More laughter*]

I'm sorry, Mooji, but my mind just keeps throwing up 'what ifs' and 'buts'! It's like I have this habit of listening to my thoughts, and I can't seem to break it! How can I make them quiet? What can I do with this noisy mind so I might know a moment's peace?

The belly of the mind is never satisfied.

Let me tell you a story ...

There was once a rich and shrewd businessman who took a holiday near a small fishing village. One morning when the sun was high and the coconut trees rocked softly in the breeze, he went for a stroll along the almost empty beach. Halfway up the beach, he came upon a small fishing boat. An old fisherman was sitting in its shade enjoying a smoke. "Good morning, friend. How come you're not out fishing? The water looks perfect for a good catch," the businessman said. "You are a man of the sea?" asked the simple fisherman. "No," answered the businessman, "but I noticed all the other boats are out except yours." "There are no other boats. I alone fish here. I fish at night. Now I take rest here in the breeze and shade," explained the old man. "But if you went out now, wouldn't you catch more fish?" "Probably. But what for?" "Well, I'm sure you could sell them all at that tourist beach over there," the business-man said, pointing towards the next village. "And then what?" asked the fisherman. "Well, then you could buy a motor for your boat and go further out to really deep waters and catch even bigger fish." "And then what?" the humble seaman asked again. "Well, then you could buy another boat, employ some of these idle young men to fish for you and so make more money!" "And what then?" said the old man. "Well, with all that money, you could build your own house. You could sit back, relax and enjoy life with a peaceful mind," responded the businessman. "Thank you for your advice," smiled the fisherman, "but that's what I am doing now." The businessman, humbled, touched his palms together and nodded in agreement.

The peace you're looking for, you already *are*. Be still, and know this.

But what about when there are things to be done, Mooji, things to be considered, actions needing to be taken?

Let actions happen without identification. In this way, actions are pure in expression. Is this so difficult? Thoughts and activity are not contrary to truth and by themselves do not impose identification. I often say this because some people have this fear that they will become spiritual vegetables, that they will stagnate and spend the rest of their lives sitting in meditation. They see personal action and striving as a virtue and imagine this type of instruction or advice as unnatural, lazy and restrictive.

But if we follow your instruction and just watch the world before us, how will anything get done?

Listen: mental, physical and emotional activities are continuously in play, the life-force is their master and originator. You, who witnesses their play, are untouched by their play. Recognise this. Impersonal perceiving of the cosmic activity free of self-interest or judgement, this itself leads to Liberation. There is immense freedom and clarity in the light of such recognition. The problem has never been how much activity there is, or even what kind of activity the body engages in. The apparent mistake is the identification of the Beingness, the Self, with the non-self. It is here that the sense of separation creeps in. With separation and an inflated sense of autonomy, comes fear, desire, restlessness and arrogance.

I say, remain as the impersonal seer: Awareness itself.

I sort of know what you are talking about, Mooji. I practice vipassana meditation, and I know that the restlessness of the mind falls away when I'm doing that. And I know a number of pranayama exercises which ...

You think you know so much, but what do you really know? You have been under the impression that you must develop skills to manage and control life, or at least, to navigate safely through it. But yourself, you remain unaware of. That, you don't know.

Can't you just let yourself be in the space of 'I don't know'? Of 'I am' without capacity to say what this 'I am' is? Can you, for now, keep the attention inside the sense of 'I am' without connecting it with any other concepts or sensations?

Can you simply rest in that natural feeling of 'I am' – without separation? Don't look for any special experience or benefit. Neither be in a state of waiting nor

31

of expectation. Recognise this unique sense of simply *being*. No further practices are necessary if you continue the inquiry with single-mindedness and devotion.

[*Silence*]

After listening to your words, I feel a little stunned ... or perhaps it is more like stoned! [Laughter] I begin to understand this much at least — that I don't really know anything at all. [More laughter]

In the land of 'I know,' there is always competitiveness, jealousy, pretence, pride and arrogance. It is an aggressive realm — the realm of the ego. I say, refuse citizenship. In the land of 'I *don't* know,' the inhabitants move without conflict and are naturally quiet, happy and peaceful.

The wise stay here.

All happens by itself

'The world is an illusion'
may not be an easy teaching,
but it is a great discovery!

You often say things like 'Don't touch that' and 'Stay neutral',
but my question is, what's wrong with engaging fully with life?
And what's so good about being neutral? It seems to me that
you're suggesting not to embrace life, not to trust our feelings,
not to bother to participate in anything — that life is a waste
of energy. But, surely this can't be what you mean?

No, not at all! Nothing is wrong with senses or with
sense objects, with any object of perception, with the
taste and touch of personality, with any sensation, or
with any of the phenomena we call life, if it is seen and
accepted as just what it is: the manifestation or play
of consciousness. The world, its experience-er and the
act or functioning of experiencing, are all the play of
the single consciousness. Seen with the pure mind,
consciousness and its ever-flowing content are neither
negative nor positive. They simply Are. The entire
manifestation is a divine play in consciousness; it is
God's *Lila,* God's creative expression.

However, it is illusory. I do not offer this to you as
a teaching, but as an invitation for you to take a closer look at what you consider to be yourself. Are you

willing to be completely open-minded throughout this investigation?

I say: Don't touch anything. This is said only to counteract the tendency or reflex to engage oneself with what is often mere mental debris, as soon as it appears in mind. It is the advice or instruction offered to serious aspirants of truth whose deepest urge is to be free from the hypnotic influence and power of the mind. By discovering the pure and immutable nature within, the spell of the mind is broken.

For those who are ready to leave all else behind for liberation from the spell of illusion, this advice comes. Others will do what they want as compelled by their nature. That, too, is the play of the cosmos and is therefore also natural. The mature seeker minds his or her own business, goes his or her own way.

But if I just do what I want ... ? What if I do something wrong or unkind? I reap the result of my wrong action, don't I? It doesn't seem right to say it is all an illusion, or that it's all just play! Or that nothing touches me or matters to me!

I am not saying that exactly — and understand that there is no arrogance behind my statement. It's more that I'm saying that the life-force itself does everything. Mind is only an interpreter. If I shoot someone in my dream, I will suffer in the dream, no doubt. Even if un-caught, in the dream, whatever my moral values may be would confront me, right there in the dream. However, when I wake up, can I be arrested in the waking state for the crime I committed in my dream? That which causes the dream to happen, would that not also be responsible for the occurrences in the dream? Can that, itself, be caught and charged with any offence? By whom? Contemplate this.

Another example: one flow of electricity is directed to this apartment. In this object, it produces heat, in that one, cool air-flow. In the television, it causes moving pictures to appear and in the fridge, it makes ice. But electricity is none of these things. It is neither hot nor cold. It has no image. If someone is killed by an electric shock, electricity cannot be charged, found guilty and sentenced to time in prison. It is neither innocent nor guilty. It is the same with the life-force and the consciousness.

If this is the case, what is the point of feeling alive, of education, creativity, evolution and striving for perfection in thought, word and deed? You make it all sound pointless!

On the contrary. The fact is, as pure understanding arises or happens – and it needn't happen suddenly, it may be gradual – the sense of a struggling personal self which we have been so accustomed to identifying as who we are: this impression or stain dissolves from our psyche and is replaced by a broader sense, by expansiveness of being. The old psychological idiosyncrasies and habits may still appear around the old snake, but now, with its fangs and venom removed, they lose force and occupy the role of a mere costume.

Selfishness, arrogance and insecurity lose their hold as the Self within is seen to be the same one Self within all beings, and effortless compassion flows outward towards all of life.

Self-inquiry

Is there some practice we have to make?

There is nothing you must do or change to *be* what you are. However, there is something you must recognise in order to *stop* being what you are not: investigate who you are. Through self-inquiry, the false sense of self, the ego, is exposed as a ghostly appearance in the light and presence of the real seer, your Self.

I know I am that. It's just that I forget easily. It feels that there is nothing one can do to help one remember ...

It is not to know or do, but to *be*.

Knowledge must be experienced. When knowledge and experience are one, there is no separation. When they are one, knowing *is* being. What is felt in the heart is counted as experience. Mind must remain in the heart.

Develop the habit of investigating yourself. Ask and seek earnestly within but don't accept answers such as 'I am this or that'. Allow the question to open up its light within your being. Be quiet and alert. Try to find out what 'I' is. 'Who or what is 'I'? Can 'I' be seen objectively? Keep quiet while watching the various forms that 'I' may assume. Sometimes, the field of vision may suddenly become blurred or blank. The 'I'-thought may vanish. But don't start celebrating!

[*Laughter*] Observe that the observing core of any activity is unmoved by any object of attention.

Now find out: what watches the sense of self?

Like this, search out the 'I'-concept and its observer relentlessly until both merge into silence. This will happen. In much the same way that great artists are ever contemplating their work, or a good detective is always thinking about solving a case – like Inspector Colombo! – the one yearning for liberation contemplates the nature of pure Self continuously, driven by some inner compulsion, until there remains only the concept-free silence of being.

All you say is crystal clear; there is so much power even in the hearing of this alone. However, my mind won't let go of the thought that there is a hurdle to jump over. Then resistance comes up and I just don't feel I have the strength to investigate ...

Engage single-mindedly in the inquiry as though your life depended on it, and this resistance will drop away in no time. The effectiveness of the inquiry is its immediacy in revealing the false as false, thus leaving the Self as the irrefutable reality. When your mind settles down in the heart, no-one will have to convince you this is your natural and original Self. As maturity grows, recognising the false, intuitively experiencing the Self, will be as swift as looking into a mirror and recognising your face. Eventually, the mind or attention will remain effortlessly in the Heart, thereby putting an end to all doubts and confusion.

Is there any scripture that backs up what you are saying here? Has any other master recommended this advice?

What I speak is nothing new, but is original in the sense that it is timeless and ever-fresh. Sages over ages have discovered this simple truth, and have pointed countless seekers towards constant investigation within so that they may come to clarify and confirm it for themselves. I say: Quit dilly-dallying. If truth is what you yearn for then go straight to the root of the matter. You won't get anywhere by sniffing around. Find out! I've shown you the way.

Step boldly into this inquiry until your doubts are removed.

*Use my words
but don't hold onto me.*

Look for yourself.

Look by yourself.

*It must all be your own
discovery.*

'That, I am'

Once there lived a king who desired enlighten-
ment. He was deeply attracted to the philosophy of
Advaita, which states that there is one undivided and all-
inclusive reality and that this is what we are. The king
loved spiritual discussions and enjoyed the company of
saints and sages.

One day a naked monk stood outside the gate of
the palace. He had very long hair and long, curling
nails and carried only a staff. He had the appearance
of a wild forest-dweller. He tapped thrice on the great
door of the palace. The guard opened the door and,
after scanning the monk from top to toe, asked: "What
do you want?"

"I have an appointment with the king," uttered
the monk.

"Wait here," replied the guard, closing the door.
"My Lord," the guard reported to the king, "there is
a naked monk outside. He says he has an appointment
with your Majesty."

The king, puzzled, instructed the guard to ask the
stranger if he was one of the royal ministers. So, the
guard returned to the door and asked the monk, "Are
you one of the king's ministers?"

The monk slowly shook his head from side to side
and, pointing his finger up towards the sky, answered,
"Higher than that."

The guard reported his answer to the king, "He says he is higher than that, your Majesty."

"Higher than a minister? Is he my councillor?"

"Are you the king's councillor?" the guard asked when he returned to the entrance of the castle.

And again, "Higher than that," came the reply.

"Your Majesty, the naked monk said again that he is 'higher than that'," the guard told the king.

"Higher than my councillor? Is he a priest? Or a prophet?" the king inquired.

"Are you a priest or a prophet?" quizzed the guard.

"Higher than that," said the pointed finger.

"Higher than a prophet?" The king straightened himself up. "Then he must be a king from another country."

"Are you a king from another country?" the guard asked, regarding the monk with some scepticism.

And, "Higher than that," again came the reply.

When the guard reported this to the king, the king drew himself up to his full height, and, gathering his robes around him, he strode down himself to the great door of the palace.

"Above the king is only God," the king declared when he saw the monk standing in the moonlight. "Are you God?"

There was a long, intense silence.

Finally, "Higher than that," uttered the monk. His eyes filled with a wild brilliance.

"What?!" exclaimed the king with surprise and awe. "Nothing is higher than God!"

A soft smile opened on the monk's radiant face. "That

... I am," came the reply.

On hearing these words, the king's energy left his body and he collapsed, unconscious, on the floor. The royal attendants brought his body to his bedroom where, for a whole week, he slept deeply. Finally, on the morning of the eighth day, he rose suddenly. The attendants brought his royal robes but the king would not put them on.

"Give them to my son," he ordered. "My work here is done. I go in search of that one who is beyond all."

Whatever concept or phenomenon
appears before you,
know that your Self,
the invisible seer,
is beyond them.

You are the unnameable,
the unborn Awareness Self.
Recognise That.
Be one with that.

You are That.

You are no thing

When you say 'Fix the attention in the Heart,' the thought comes: "No matter what I do, I am identifying with an 'I'."

It is enough to know that when the sense 'I am' is recognised phenomenally, something more subtle lies behind and beyond. Looking for this 'something' which lies beyond, no objective entity is found. The seeker and the sought merge in one-ness and all that remains is boundless silence and intuitive presence. The advice of those who realise this is: "Be There. Be That."

Now, is there something left to say?

[Long silence]

There's a kind of total I ...

Why call it 'I'? What rushes forward to name it?

Trace to the root this urge or tendency to label, evaluate or qualify perception. At the crucial point of recognition, a wordless instant, something springs up: "Yes, there is an I, a total I," or some such remark. Don't identify with that thought. Instead, investigate: what makes this response? It will become clear that it springs out of nothing, nothing at all.

If left unquestioned, the hypnosis of identity will remain undiscovered. Investigate your assumptions until they are exposed and recognised as merely thoughts, all of them, including the 'one' who appears to be affected by them. Yes! This emotional, psychological 'I' is also a thought. Throughout the life of this body, something has been saying "I" millions of times. Yet, when asked: "Who or what is 'I'?" – none can say.

Real self-discovery is the recognition and realisation of what this 'I' is. The whole-hearted realisation that 'I' is the supreme Self and not a 'person' is what is called Liberation. And crucially, vagueness about 'I' is the ace-card up the sleeve of the mind and is often missed or overlooked.

'I' is the master-thief itself. This is the thief Sri Ramana speaks about, dressed in the policeman's uniform to go out to catch the thief – who is himself! Of course, the thief will not be caught. This policeman-thief will run around, blow his whistle and pretend he is earnestly seeking the thief, but he won't ever put himself in jail. Ego won't and can't kill ego. So this thief, who is it? This I of I's is also a thought – the most intimate and primal thought in creation.

I think I have several identities playing simultaneously. I regard each as a part of the one self I am.

Whatever ideas you may hold about yourself, however profound, however accurate or objective you consider them to be, they cannot be true, cannot contain, convey or represent that which you are. Ideas, feelings and opinions are variable, they cannot be more stable than their observer. Bring your attention away from the objects of perception and rest it on the witnessing awareness alone. Who are you here and now?

I am nothing.

Yes, you are no 'thing'. You are no-body. When the attention is turned towards its source, it is clear and fearless, this realisation. If you say to most people, "You are nobody," they would feel hurt or insulted. "Why do you say that? Who do you think you are talking to?" they would cry. But if you say to a sage, "You are nobody, you are nothing" – he will reply: "Thank you for reminding me," although, in truth, he is beyond reminding.

My Master often said: "You need nothing to be happy – you need something to be sad." As long as you are invested in the world of something-ness, of another trip, another book, another angle to view life, your vision is shaped and influenced by the conditioned mind. Therefore, you seem one, two, three steps removed from yourself. Of course this is not true, but it will feel true to you, because you place that which you are at the end of some striving. The mind tricks you easily with some promise because you are eager to co-operate with its suggestions. True insight springs from emptiness.

So again, right now, what are you clinging to?

The idea that something needs to be done.

'Something needs to be done' is also a thought, a very familiar and believable thought. We rarely question such thoughts for our culture prepares us to strive and struggle for what is in reality the most natural; for what is already so. It paints self-discovery, self-awareness, into a poetic fantasy or a strenuous striving. Therefore, the need to 'act', to 'do', to 'strive' towards a far-off goal, seems natural and even noble. A voice we know says: "All this sounds true. I will do some research, learn something about this new philosophy. It gives many great insights and teachings, the best I've heard. It will, no doubt, help me on my journey." And you believe it straight away, unquestioned. So, inevitably, in that instant, the waters divide; the sense of separation is wedged in more tightly.

You are like the empty space in which the wind roams around. The nature of wind is to move from place to place, but space is infinite and still, and, being infinite, incapable of even the slightest movement. There cannot be wind without space but there can be space without wind. Space is not troubled by the activity of the wind; neither gentle breeze nor hurricane affects it in the least. Similarly, you, the Self, are boundless and unmoving like space, but you identify with the movements of the wind-mind playing inside you, and forget your real nature.

Sometimes, the mind blows like a tornado. How can I calm it? It seems impossible. Even meditation doesn't help.

Even if wind turns into a tornado, how could it affect or disturb space? Contemplate this. You meditate and do all sorts of things to make your mind more quiet. Let me ask: Is space more space-like when no wind blows?

Knowing this is to free oneself from illusory efforts to control the wind-mind. Be space and let mind roam where it wills. This is the secret my master revealed to me. Remain as the ever-present Awareness. To know and understand mind is to transcend mind. Mind is wind and wave; Self is ocean or space. Identify 'I' as ocean, as space, not as wave or cloud, and instantly, you are out of the 'I'-trap. Better still, identify with nothing and remain as you are. No one can remove 'I', therefore, accept 'I' as God and everything is included inside it. Where there is only one, no fear can exist. Take 'I' to be the impersonal Self and not the personal ego.

What remains now?

Nothing ... only ... some feelings arising ...

Yes, now your words come from the true. Remain as the nothingness. Let thoughts arise, but don't nurse them, because if you say, "Now I have to let feelings arise," the mind can quickly turn that into another task again.

Actually, my heart is in total peace.

The attention has merged with the source, the Self. There is neither interest nor disinterest. There is a state of effortless detachment. Therefore, you are happy.

When you engage your attention with anything, you give it life.

This is not to say you must not enjoy beautiful flowers, the beach, the sun, fine food, nor that the choice between having a sleep or a swim should not be made. Be clear about this. The play of choice is a natural expression of the self in manifestation. Be natural, be yourself in every situation with everything, be at ease with everything! Only recognise that whatever manifests in consciousness is a playful and superficial expression and not a definition of what you are. It may be the playing-out of the conditioning on the body-mind level, but *you* are deeper and beyond all definitions. Stay here.

You and me

I struggle with the ideas of 'you' and 'me'.

Let 'you' and 'me' be there. Find out who you are first!

When we see clearly that we are one …

What do you mean? In what way are we one?

We share everything …

Share means two or more. We? What is this 'we'? What is a person? What do we share? When you look into another person, what is it, what do you see?

A bundle of illusion, sufferings, dreams …

[*Silence*]

You can have a life called 'spiritual,' but still you may live in ignorance. Who Are You? This is the most auspicious question that can present itself. Don't walk away from it. Many find it highly irritating. Perhaps this is why so few come to my satsangs. [*Laughter*] In the beginning, I thought thousands would come, climbing over each other for freedom, but … where are they? Who really wants freedom?

If you take yourself to be 'I', a person, you will take others to be 'you', 'him', and 'her', other persons. That's why this saying stands true: "I don't see the world as it is, I see the world as I am." This entire world, comprising its perceiver, is a great seeming.

Look into this 'I' you take yourself to be. You don't know how you know anything. We don't know what knowledge is, and we don't know what there is to know. I ask: What is the foundation of mind itself? Out of what is mind arising?

Don't think, don't imagine. Just look! Stay with this investigation. When you pursue this question with determination, it will feel like you are on the back of a wild horse. But stay there. Mind is being witnessed. What witnesses mind?

If our basic assumptions about who we are remain unchallenged, mind will be our identity. Something is prior to mind, watches mind, knows its vibration.

What is that?

Can it be other than you?

[*Silence*]

Go for Gold

Very often, thoughts come but they don't carry us away. Why? Because we have no particular interest in them. We struggle only with thoughts and feelings which have meaning for us. Only after we have formed personal relationship with them can they command and engage our attention. This leads to a subtle state of hypnosis in which our attention has hooked into a flow of thoughts and feelings which can quickly escalate into an emotional state of confusion and restlessness. We feel we are suffering, that we are distracted from the true Self. But can we not also perceive this pull on our attention? At this point we are not, as yet, inside the dreaming mind, we are its observer. If we don't 'log in', as it were, the throb of thoughts will quickly subside or pass on.

We need not panic nor be afraid of thoughts, for thought-activity is the natural display of the life-force in its expression through the human form. It is our mistaken identification with the root-thought, the 'I'-thought, that allows other thoughts tenancy in our being. The Self-seeker develops the habit of observing without entering the phenomena arising as mind. He uses the thoughts themselves, formerly the offending particles, to expose their supposed subject: the

53

ego-self. When, eventually, the seed-thought that is the ego is strained out, pure seeing remains. Self is the sole seer.

How can we attain that state? Thoughts seem so unrelenting.

Remain as the space-like intelligence which sees without personal interest or engagement. Being formless, it is incapable of association. Recognise its presence; it is already here. Be one with it.

The attention drifts off-course easily.

Each time the attention runs out, bring it back inside where it merges with awareness. There might be a little resistance and discomfort in the beginning but this will gradually settle down as the silence comes to the foreground. This is the fruit of detached or passive observing. It gradually becomes effortless and natural, ripening into an unbroken state of space, peace and joy. Detachment exposes the personal identity as a myth. It leaves the self in a state of passive and panoramic perceiving, free from the burden caused by personalised seeing. Gradually, the vast superstructure of conditionings and concepts that appeared to have covered the beingness begin deconstructing until their concealing power is neutralised.

Don't limit yourself to any state, however pleasing. Don't settle for bronze. By 'bronze', I mean spiritual knowledge, short-lived blissful states and paranormal experiences. Find the one substratum of all these states

– unmoving, undivided, unaffected by events in time and space. Go for Gold!

And I thought that you have been telling us not to go any-where, that we are already there! [Laughter]

This is the one and only race you will win by going absolutely nowhere! [*Laughter*]

Tell me, why, throughout the ages, man has used the symbol of gold to represent the highest? 'In Gold we trust' some even say! Is it not because gold is incorruptible? In this case, 'gold' means unalloyed, impersonal seeing/being. It means purity beyond the concept of purity.

This is not a lofty, unattainable goal, a reward for your good conduct or strenuous practices. It is what you cannot help but be: the only reality you already are!

Remain fixed in the heart.
Whenever and wherever the attention goes,
bring it back to Awareness Self.

Gradually, it will remain there without effort.

This is the only practice one need do.

Full Stop

I know I am not what appears in the consciousness, that I am the witness and formless. Nevertheless, the force of the mind-stuff continues to throb and doesn't seem to be subsiding.

This knowledge is what I call 'un-swallowed food.' It is mental, and not the full experience of truth. If, as you say, you are the witness only, and we have seen that the witness is impersonal and formless, who will be there to be affected or disturbed by any mind-stuff?

No-one. But ...

Stop there! Where is the place for 'but'? Who says 'but ... '? Who even says: 'no-one'? Can any answer be correct?

There is no answer to the question 'Who am I'. Why? Because that question is a subjective one, a search for the subject, and it cannot be satisfied by an objective response. The subject, that which I truly am, cannot be contained or conveyed by an answer, which is merely a concept.

The questioner, along with any answer, should be discovered as the mind, as a thought, and can thus be rejected as false, as an object in the view of the conceiver. I am that which witnesses mind, therefore I am earlier, more subtle than thought and entirely formless.

Therefore when you say 'no-one,' you are to stop at that; sink into that and be one with that. Enter and rest in the evidence of your own discovery which reveals: 'No-one, am I.'

Nothing alone Is. This is the confirmation. After this subtle intuitive recognition, all subsides into emptiness. Emptiness alone remains. Know you are That.

There is no you

There are some areas in which my attention gets caught, for example in the relationship with my family.

Whatever engages your attention becomes your experience. There is a kind of easiness with getting involved, and the result is that you feel yourself to be a 'somebody.'

Why does this happen?

Attention goes because of habit. I think that all the questions around spirituality boil down to this point. Something from your past engages your attention and this leads to a state of agitation, and you make some effort to manipulate the agitation or suppress it, in order to change it.

When we see that that is the past playing out, can we just let it go?

This seems a very good question. If I continue along the line of this particular question, I'm cooperating with an idea which is not true, that there's a 'you' who lives your life. If you think you are a 'someone' acting from your past, you are reinforcing this mistaken identity.

Find who it is that sees things in that way. Who is the one acting and reacting? Is there really an actual 'I' who has this conditioning?

Don't ask merely in order to get rid of the conditioning or the discomfort, but to really see if that is what you are. See that which has no family; it's not a woman or a man, and has no past. Go beyond all association until you alone remain without *you*.

The problem is not the role itself, but the belief in it.

Yes. But ... for example, in my family, they see me as a person.

You have no control over what others think and do. You will only create a burden trying to fix this. Just be honest and true in the moment. Look, 'I' has some past associations, future projections, role or behaviour, and because of the belief in the role, consciousness is held hostage in a certain identity.

Who is 'I' and precisely where is 'I' right now? Can I be any thing? What would that be? Such questions guide consciousness back to emptiness, its source. Satsang presents the chance to recognise your Self directly, to discover that which is timeless and unchangingly present.

Why do we forget our nature?

What we really are doesn't forget. It is not capable of remembering and forgetting.

* * *

I made a wrong move.

I don't know anything as a wrong move. Everything is just perfect! This idea is holding you hostage and it is a complete fabrication of your mind!

Stop thinking that you produce yourself. There is no actual, factual you, nothing there at all, except as an idea. The seer of this is the single reality we are. Mind perceives emptiness as absence of activity, powerlessness, personal non-existence; it doesn't realise that emptiness is purity, peace and complete satisfaction of being. Even now, this is so. Even now, as you put these questions. The one who speaks is the one who listens.

There is a stage in this inquiry which can feel quite paranoid, when even the subtlest of sensations is inquired into. Gradually this kind of zealousness subsides and only inquiry is left, without an inquirer. Who is inquiring? No one is inquiring.

This cannot be understood rationally. In truth, this cannot be explained, and you cannot find yourself because you have never been separated. Paradox and riddles exist only for the mind. You are that which contains all paradoxes.

* * *

You told me, "Don't look with the mind, look with the heart." I don't know how to look with the heart.

Who is this 'I' that says, "I don't know how to look with the heart"?

Forget about anything you have heard or read. Forget about all this. I'm not expecting that there's any 'you' who will understand and remember this. It's like a ball of wool that has been tangled up, and each time it comes here to satsang it's all "Oh, how did I become entangled like this?"

An explanation seems to be given to it, but the explanation is only another way of bouncing it against the wall, and it untangles by itself. The ball cannot receive the advice 'How I can untangle myself.' What must happen is that that I, as Stillness itself, hold it, and it runs until it is unravelled – but itself is not able to carry out that advice!

This should be very unburdening for you. You don't have to do anything whatsoever. These dialogues are a kind of play; it's not really what's going on. The cooking is happening underneath somehow. Whatever needs to happen is happening by itself. Just look.

The only thing I can describe is what I can see. Therefore, what I can see, it's happening to me.

What is aware of this happening?

Each time you follow this question is like a mirror reflecting you-looking-at-this-activity and the mirror itself. How close is the reflection? However close it is, it's never going to turn into you, because you're seeing the reflection.

Everything is just now. Your existence is just now. Just timeless Now. All the rest is a dream due to conditioning and memory.

Whose memory? No one's memory. It is a mystery! A mystery cannot be worked out. "For whom is the mystery?" is the most important question. Find out!

Try this:

*Right now, don't touch any idea about
progress, future, or self-evaluation,*

*and don't expect anything at all
from what is taking place now.*

Make no effort, for just this moment.

What remains?

There is no 'way' to be

I feel like I still watch a lot of the movie.

Something is viewing the watching of the movie. Be completely clear. In listening to the mind you sometimes create a sense that there is a certain way to be.

There is no way to be. You are. It is enough, full stop. But you must find out what this 'you are,' meaning 'I am,' is. The expression is this 'I am-ness', it is the language of the waves flowing on the surface of the ocean. Ocean is being – wave is mind. Waves are inseparable from the ocean. They are there, and they are one. Both are water only, it is the mind that sees wave and ocean; Beingness merely sees.

What you do, the way you move, your likes and dislikes, belong to this form and are therefore natural. They don't affect your real nature. You like ballet, someone else likes hip-hop; that's your thing, enjoy it. It's not in these matters that you go in search of what you are! Even your questioning arises out of this manifestation. It is dancing by itself. It's not 'you' doing it! Who is making the waves move?

This is felt somehow. But I see that there is still a judgement that operates through thinking. This judgement, where does it come from? This identity is kept somehow, you know?

Kept by what?

As belief.

As belief, good. Whose belief?

Nobody's belief. Just belief in the mind.

Stay put right there, otherwise the profundity of what you've just uttered will turn nicely into philosophy.

[*Silence*]

Be one with that recognition. Don't leave it as mere comment. "It's nobody's belief," you say. Belief is also perceived. You stay put here, and it's as though a wave of emptiness washes away all dirt from the mind.

Nobody can say what this emptiness is. Yet, when recognised, it is the inescapable ground of all that appears or exists. Know this deep in your heart so that it becomes inseparable from what you are.

That is the crucial point, you see. Even if you should spend one thousand more years in spiritual training, you will eventually have to come back to this point that we are right now and right here. Why waste a thousand years? Face the one that wants to run away, for it is a trickster and a thief who, if unquestioned and untraced, will keep you on the wheel of existence – of *samsara*. Knowing this, would you willingly allow yourself to be tricked out of eternal freedom?

This doubt is very strong in the mind and I am striving because I want to see it clearly.

'It' being what? It is simply the very seeing itself. The saying 'What you are searching for is where you are searching from,' is it true or isn't it?

[*Silence*]

If the mind keeps this idea that there is a kind of ultimate 'It' to reach through practice, it will then imagine the Self as some elusive phenomenon or some image that will always be just out of reach or completely unattainable. Like this, the journey for ultimate truth is turned into an almighty epic or a journey of severe hardships.

As the soup 'thickens,' we experience moments of clarity and real peace. We are further encouraged by occasional 'glimpses' of the beingness. We rarely question if these experiences are actually of the Self or an illusory projection of the mind. The idea that we might already be the Self we are searching for is hardly ever considered.

This becomes very clear. I've been looking for something for a long time. And then I saw that I could have never seen anything because the seeing alone is the only thing that was there. Whatever I would have seen would have been a phenomenon.

You stop right here, now. There's nothing more to chew. All this has brought you here.

I am always quick to ask "What is the trouble here?" Because if you've been in prison for ten years and then you're set free, and you come out and start lamenting,

"Why did I spend so long in prison?" – this shows you are still in prison!

These thoughts come to you again and again because they get five-star service. [*Laughter*] I call them thief-thoughts. Papaji says, "Let them be like thieves in an empty house."

The most precious thing you have right now is your attention. The body grows with food and exercise. Mind grows with belief, intention and interest. But this 'I' also is growing through the sense of identity with and interest in the body. If it is not contaminated through identity with the body-mind functioning, it stays as neutral perceiving.

In just the same way, if you're driving in some panoramic space, you're taking in a broad field of impressions but not landing on anything. There is a sort of neutrality in that.

There is still a habit of giving importance to some things more than others. I can see that this is because the attention is used to residing on those things because they have held meaning and importance.

Once you have really come to this place of clear seeing and it is recognised that there is no actual person 'giving importance to things' except as an idea that arises quite naturally in consciousness, the poison is then taken out of the serpent. You don't have to kill him. He will die by himself if he needs to.

Life dances as the spontaneous expression arising out of this.

It requires no story teller; it simply is. This body will behave spontaneously and appropriately to the needs of the moment. The sense of duality is still present, but again, you are not a prisoner of it.

This state is inscrutable. No-one can lay down rules or tracks for it. There are no maps for being. In every expression, it is the sole presence and core. You are That.

Only the one with perfect eyes
can see Perfection.

And what are perfect eyes?

Eyes that see
without desire or interpretation.

Arunachala
The holy mountain of Tiruvannamalai, South India

Mooji with Sri Yogi Ramsuratkumar, 1994

Who is living your life?

Today I went for a second operation on my eyes. The first time I went, I thought I had been very good, very still and calm. There was an 'I' who was achieving this state. This second time there was only the sensation of an 'I' trembling in ... this. It was like air seeing all this. There wasn't a somebody watching the 'I' reacting.

This seeing is Being, and this experiencing is Being, all one thing.

... When I was given the command to keep my sight on the flashing light, I thought that if I had carried on just giving my attention to this space behind, instead of falling into that 'I' with all its investment in what was going on, I wouldn't have been able to follow the instructions that would make the operation possible, that would keep it safe.

We think that the 'I' cannot operate if Wholeness alone *is*. It shows that there's something that feels the 'I' is necessary. Some say that the ego is necessary to be in the world. Who is it that is living your life, taking care of your family, making sure bills are paid – if there is no 'I'? Somehow consciousness is responsible for all this play, and in order to have the experience of itself, it dreams individuality, to have the illusion of having a life.

But it seems necessary for 'Joan' [questioner's name] to be dreamt up for that story to happen ... ?

Does it make you feel that you are Joan? What's the result of seeing that Joan is an event of consciousness? All manifestations of life, variety, contrasts, etc., necessarily create the sense of an 'I' in order to experience the sense of others. Duality is a necessary power for manifestation to happen. Time and space are necessary constructions for things to appear and to move. In this, are you hammered into a role, for example, 'Joan's'?

Yes, in a way it feels like that. It seems that in me the consciousness only tells Joan's story. This feels like a limitation.

If this legitimate Joan is taken to be an autonomous entity, then you have misunderstood. Look at who or what is Joan. What is she constructed of?

... But if a story has to be told here, it can be only through Joan.

It's not that. You're assuming still a great volume for this Joan. It's like saying that all you are experiencing is Joan seeing. Actually there is no Joan. Something wants to relate to her because she feels intimate and actual. When I relate to you, I relate only as consciousness. Look for Joan!

[Long silence] ... There is nothing there.

Keep looking and seeing that there is nothing there. Stop thinking that 'you' produce Joan. Let others talk to you about her, but yourself, you won't be able to find this one. There is no name for you, except as an idea.

[*Silence*]

Thank you.

What if one cannot find a Master?

The real Master is within you.
It is your innermost reality.

It is not your mind.

Mind hides the Master.

When mind is there, Master is not;
when Master is there, mind is not.

When two masters meet ...

Mooji, what happens when two masters meet? What would you talk about if you met another master?

They may say: "How guru do?" [*Big laughter*]
Whatever will happen, will happen. As for being a master, when I look within, I don't find any 'master' here. We entertain all kind of fanciful notions that some cosmic shift should happen, like bringing two big magnets together, and this is nonsense. They are no two masters meeting. What is the difference between the space in this room and the space in the kitchen? None at all. So, whatever will happen would not register to them as an event, because in truth nothing is happening. Nothing happens!

But surely there must be some recognition between them?

Recognition between whom?

Between the two of them, of course. Perhaps an interest in each other's way of expressing 'This'! For their truth is one, but the teaching is many. Within all cultures, there is a spectrum of modes of conveying the unveiling of the obvious, so to speak, but also a unique philosophic perennis, *that each initiates words in a peculiar way. They should enjoy this diversity.*

You don't know what you are saying or how things are. If they are 'masters' as you say, they wouldn't hold any such concept of themselves as masters. That principle which you refer to as master wears no concept of itself. Free from all 'I'-belief, it exists as awareness only. The true Master has no teaching, he or she merely points the way. No teaching, no student, no master. [*Smiles*] This is the truth taught by all masters to their disciples, isn't it?

Then what are we doing here? What is the purpose of satsang?

To find this out; discovering and confirming this for yourself.

But aren't these just the usual zen-like phrases that many Advaita teachers use? 'No teacher, no teaching, no student,' it doesn't ring true for me. It seems clear to me that you are the teacher and I am here benefiting from your teaching and your presence. What is the value or point in saying this isn't so? I enjoy coming here and being with you. Your words and presence have clearly helped me. Surely, you love teaching or, let's say, sharing what you have found. Wouldn't you say teaching is your role in life? Your presence seems stronger than ours. You speak with more authority and clarity than anyone I know. I love and respect you. Do you not feel the same for us? How do you perceive us, the ones who come to you?

Don't place me on a pedestal and don't box me in. I am not what you perceive me to be. There is nothing objective I can say about myself that can remain true.

I've looked and found no objective location for what I am. I know I am aware and perception is happening within my self spontaneously, but there isn't a 'someone' there doing or achieving something. There is no difference between 'you' and 'me,' except that I know that I am not a 'person' and you feel you are. I try my best to challenge, confront, stimulate, inspire and encourage you in order that you may see and confirm it for yourself. I cannot help doing this, it just happens.

Teacher and student are roles and forms appearing in the consciousness we are, as it is expressing itself. Why and how consciousness does it, I don't know. And I don't need to know. Somehow, it seems to me that consciousness creates this play in order to have the experience of awakening to itself as the pure, immutable reality. That is its joy. Self assumes all these masks. Self forgets itself, and in that it seems to discover its Self. Yet it remains pure Self all along. This is my view.

When it dreams itself to be the individual 'I', the 'me', it manifests as a separate entity, restless and arrogant, unaware of its true nature. Under the spell of its own *Maya*, it is prone to feelings of fear and resistance, doubt and anxiety. As 'me,' it suffers; it can't avoid suffering and struggling, because we all have this intuition that our individual existence is bound to end. This I call the 'trauma of existence.' Still, the Self is slow in giving up its arrogance, its identity as 'me.' Why? Even here in satsang, people are often prideful and arrogant. Somehow, when the beingness gets stressed enough and tired of it all, and when it chooses to wake up, the mind-force backs off, as it were, while the pull towards truth and satsang increases.

In all of this, there is no 'do-er.' No one 'do-ing' or 'un-doing' anything, all happens by itself. This is what one observes, and a great unburdening takes place, real peace and joy prevail as a result of this recognition.

You ask: "Do you love to teach?" I have no agenda to teach and don't feel I am actively teaching anyone or anything. I am just doing my 'thing', dancing my dance. It is all completely spontaneous. I am 'enjoy-ing' my self in all its expressions, rough or smooth. While the body is here, the dancing goes on. Somehow, everything is fine and harmonious around me, for I know that nothing can go wrong, except in some superficial and temporary aspects.

I enjoy the satsang salsa, but I'm not attached to it. Though it may appear so, I am not attached to anyone or anything. If I had to walk away and leave all of my present life behind, I would be totally fine. When and if it falls away, I am remaining as emptiness – even now this is so. I am emptiness walking in the guise of a human being called Mooji.

Presence, stillness, clarity and authority prevail when mind is transcended, seen through, and understood as the play of waves on the ocean's face. One realises and identifies as Self only. This is the Divine attraction, the divine romance. Like the butterflies are drawn towards the buddleia flower, all the beings who are ready to

wake up come to bathe in the ocean of peace and compassion. Their minds re-integrate with Source, thus the
yoga of knowledge and understanding is consummated.
This is the play, the satsang play.

Now, you ask as well, "How do you see us?" And
I say: As forms of the One-ness in expression. This is
not some mystical, effortful, heady or sentimental
sense of the manifest world, but the natural and simple
way that is felt and confirmed when the mind is not in-
terfering any more, not projecting nor taking account.
Compassion replaces fear. I stopped fearing you and
began loving you as forms of my very Self, because the
understanding came.

Self has nothing but love for Self.

The mind is ever-seeking new lands to explore
in the search for satisfaction,
picking up new burdens along the way.

Restless for change, hungry for adventure,

it misses its one real refuge –

the Self

from which it arises.

The only thief in the universe

Mooji, this search for myself seems to be taking a long time ...
sometimes, it feels like I'm going crazy! There are still so many
thoughts, all racing around in my head, sometimes I just can't
get behind them ... Finding peace feels like a dream ...

Don't be willing to touch anything that slows you
down. Let everything go, now! It's time. You have
spent lots of energy, lots of attention, lots of power, on
things which are not going anywhere. You have given
a tremendous amount of energy to trivial things. Why
don't you give a little of your time to explore 'What am
I without all these things?'

Here, in satsang, it feels fine, but out there, in my daily life ...

This is already a concept. It is not true. This which you
are cannot 'go'. It is your attention that goes elsewhere!
My challenge to everybody is this: Right here, right
now, step out of this Here-Now – and tell me when you
come to some edge where here becomes there, and now
becomes then. Give your attention to this. In this Here-
Now, racing thoughts can manifest, even craziness can
manifest, but racing craziness can only be detected
from This, which itself is not craziness! Within this
space-like emptiness, you see that when 'life' comes,

it's only thoughts and conditionings behaving, being observed also from Here and Now.

Allow yourself this freedom. Say: "My life can be totally chaotic!" Don't touch the feeling that you have lost anything and you will experience a great freedom from experiencing turbulently. 'Turbulent' is not even how you will speak of experience anymore. You will fire the internal journalist, let everything happen as it does, and you will meet everything from this emptiness ... Then tell me what difficulty you have!

How do I fire this internal journalist?

First of all, don't entertain this idea of 'how to?' because it will bite you. How do you drop a hot potato? When you are curious, you learn, but when you are desperate – you discover!

You believe that the architect-mind has to decide everything. But there is a deeper mind, the cosmic-mind, doing everything perfectly. This thing of 'how to do ... ?', and racing thoughts, and feelings of guilt and regret, will all leave. *Tamasic* energy is swallowed up by *rajasic* energy, and *raja* is swallowed by *sattva*, and then *sattva* is mutated into total presence!

This search for complete understanding cannot be a part-time job – but this doesn't mean that you have to give up your day job! Actually, you will find that everything that needs to be done happens more efficiently when the sense of a do-er falls away. In your daily life, carry on with what you have to do, because it was never about this. If you stop being a chef and become a priest, it isn't going to help you to be more you. No demand is put on you to shave your head, buy sandals, wear white clothes ... nothing like this. As you are in your life – it's holy as it is! Right here, right now, you are the Buddha itself – the Buddha in jeans! [*Laughter*]

* * *

When you discover who this 'I' is, you don't need to ask any more questions. Whatever arises for you, this entire world, is only appearing in your consciousness. Everything arises: you must be there to perceive it. 'I' is the common denominator of all experiences. So, who is this 'I'? Why is this the most auspicious question? Because without questioning who this 'I' is, you already take yourself to be a person; you take this body to be what you are. Whatever role 'I' plays, the watcher of 'I' is earlier, stable and imageless. Recognise and remain as that 'I'-less intuition.

Somehow Beingness is manifesting in such a way that it seems we are sucked into identification with an individual body. In satsang you're asked 'Who are you?' and it feels confusing because you have never been asked this question before. We know objective questions only, like, 'How far is Japan from Israel?' or 'How does this work?' This is *objective* knowledge. Now you're asked: 'Who are you who knows this knowledge?' And you say, "It's me, of course, what kind of question is this ... ?"

What comprises this 'me'? What does it make you, this 'me'?

Ummm ... lots of things ... There's me, my mind, my body ...

Yes, but what says '*my* mind,' what knows that?

... I notice these things ...

Who is the 'I' who notices them? You have just reported these things you notice, the 'me,' 'my memory', 'my conditioning', 'my feelings', 'my body' and so on – phenomena. Something is able to notice them. Who or what is it that notices them? Find that source in yourself – *while* the noticing is happening ...

It happens here ... [questioner gestures at the area around the body]

What recognises that it happens *here*? Where is that? If something surrounds *you*, as you indicate, you must be some form, no?

I'm a spirit.

But has it a form, if it is surrounded? 'Surrounding' is a kind of feeling – who is the 'me' that feels surrounded? Is it an object? Is it a male or a female?

I'm many things ... all of it. I'm this heart beating ...

What knows that? Where would you say this intelligence come from?

It should be from the mind ...

What is saying, "It should be from the mind?"

[*Questioner laughs and throws up hands, indicating 'giving up'*]

Let's go back to this 'I' you speak about.

Okay ... When I'm here, I feel peace, I feel relieved from agitation. But when I'm away from here, my attention seems to go outward, and I seem not to be aware of what's behind. Here in satsang, when I turn my attention inwards, I see that I am that emptiness. Emptiness is there.

And can you find a 'me' distinct from emptiness? Is there a 'you'?

[*Silence*]

If you perceive a 'you' in emptiness, must that not necessarily be a kind of objective quality, to which you are prior, of which you are the observer?

When your attention turns towards This, it has already been seen by This. Attention itself is a quality of the mind, and it is also being observed. This 'I-am-turning-towards-this' is what you *believe* you are – an entity that does something and gets something in return.

A feeling of joy is present when you remember and turn towards this! But there is that in which whether your 'I' turns or doesn't turn, it doesn't make any difference. When this understanding is caught – by whom? by nobody! – then the somebody who caught it disappears into no-body-ness!

All is a thought arising in this! 'Oh, but that's deep! ...' is also a thought being perceived. Lots of fears coming up? Also triggered or energised by thought! The tendency to identify with an I-who-does-some-thing? Also a thought. As long as the body is there and the life-force is in it, the potential for thought-activity is latent ...

Like so, the feeling 'I' can be there, as long as the body is here and the life-force is in it, but the poison has been taken out. The 'I'-thought – the only thief in the universe – has been exposed, and the nature of any illusion is that when it is exposed as an illusion, it loses its power.

*There is no answer
to the question 'Who am I?'*

*When one searches for the root
of the 'I' thought,
the seeker is itself exposed
and proven as a myth.*

*This results in the dissolution
of the sense of separateness
and the ultimate recognition of Truth,
the imageless background
of all appearances.*

*Awareness is the Unchanging,
in which all arises
and is perceived
as an ephemeral play.*

Wherever there is identity,
there is an 'I' entity.

Find out what this 'I' entity is.

See if it is real.

Who are you? – I am

Mooji, you always throw the 'Who-are-you?'-question in our face ... so now I ask you: 'Who are you?'

I am the timeless, the unchanging, the Real.

Where did you come from?

From nowhere.

But you are here!

Yes, ever so.

Why have you come?

The question 'why?' is irrelevant. I have never come, I will never go; I am existence beyond any reason or cause; I am, beyond the mind and its world, just like you.

But I can see you, sitting here before me!

Yes, before the 'me,' I am. What you see is not what I am.

I don't understand ...

You cannot understand Truth, you can only know it by realising that you are Truth itself.

Don't think the mind will help you. Its job is to confuse you and to raise doubt in you — a job it does very well. [*Laughter*] The only thing is that it needs your co-operation to deceive you — a job *you* do very well. [*Laughter*]

It is a game. This is why it is called *Lila* — God's play. It is your own *Maya* playing with you.

Thoughts come and go, Being does not. *You* witness thoughts. You are the unmoving screen on which thoughts are perceived, and you are the perceiver of them also — this is the riddle of existence. As long as you identify with ego-mind, you miss the obvious — your own formless presence.

How can I find it, this presence you're speaking of?

It cannot be 'found'. It simply is, and you are that already. Can you draw a line between you and Being? Find first the one who tries to find anything. Afterwards, see if there is still something to find.

But I don't actually know what 'formless presence' is!

Of course you don't! It cannot be 'known' either. Who is searching? What is it that wants to know?

Me!

Okay, and what is 'me'? Introduce yourself.

All of it: my body, my mind, my thoughts, desires also, my soul …

Who or what says this? Who sees this? Before they reached your mouth, out of what did these words emerge? You hand me a list of things, you say: 'my' body. I say: *Whose* body? Does it belong to you like your car or your clothes? You say also: 'my mind,' don't you? Meaning it's *yours*, not *you*. Even 'my soul' you say: 'my soul is rejoicing' or 'my soul was heavy with grief ... ' Soul is changing, you remain behind, you witness what happens in your soul, so — what are *you*?

... me, myself ...

Prior to thoughts and words and their arising, that which neither precedes nor follows them, what is that? Don't touch this 'me,' it's just a word, it's a concept. Look. Don't think. Be still. Observe.

... Nothing ... I see nothing at all!

No-Thing is correct. No-Thing meaning formless, beyond form, beyond time. You are not a 'thing,' how could you be? Any thing, mental or physical, appears, floats by or swims, through your consciousness. And we are the witness of this consciousness, its content and activity. Can you confirm this?

... Yes ... yes ... so I am the same as you?

Yes. Only remove the thought: 'the same as.'

I am you.

Yes. [*Pause*] And what about deleting the 'you?' Can't you do that?

[*Long silence*]

When you said 'I am you,' did the word 'you' refer to Mooji? Do you refer to this body sitting on this chair? [*Mooji shakes his body like a kind of puppet*] Is this body Mooji? Who is Mooji? This body is not different from that body or all other bodies [*pointing to people in the room*], it is made of the elements and is elemental food. Worms or fire are waiting for it. Is it what you are?

Many mystics say such things: 'All are One, I am you, you are me, no difference ... ' but if it's not your experience, it's just words for you, hollow words, and that can be felt straight away. Better not to say anything, keep quiet. So, again, what are you?

I Am.

Yes, very good. Now, drop the 'I Am.'

[*Long silence*]

Who is to delete the 'I am'?

You tell me!

[*Questioner smiles*] ... *If I am nothing, then nothing deletes anything, deleting happens.*

This is so. Very true.

Now, don't even bother about 'deleting' and 'happenings'. Don't pick up any arrogance. Don't pick up any idea.

Don't pick up anything at all.

We feel,
sometimes,
we lose or leave our self.

But this 'I' who leaves is the mind only – a thought.

How can we, being one, leave our Self?
Can the wave-mind exist apart from the ocean-Self?

'Losing and gaining' are notions arising
in the Unchanging Awareness

we already are.

You are fired!

Reject the idea of a one, or someone, who is doing the looking and living, and let the looking and living be. That deceptive 'me' is imagined into existence in order to make duality spicy. It creates much mischief until it is finally recognised and understood to be illusory. Leave it be – it is not what you are.

Don't get rooted in ego, break off from this 'I-me' sense by constantly recognising it as a phenomenon appearing in the space of your self, the unchanging reality. Physical senses will still function, perceiving will still occur. But intentions are not needed. Don't offer any tenancy to the personal 'I'-ego. Scrutinise it, find and hold it, if you can: *who am I?* What arises as 'I' here inside the body? Is it tangible? If so, to whom? Find this out. The very attempt to catch hold of it breaks its spell and thus leaves you as pure self-awareness.

So unsparing is the inquiry, so immediate at exposing the ego-sense in us as an apparition, as unreal! Inquiry is not a teaching. I say it is like looking into a mirror. The mirror will not teach you anything. It neither judges nor complains. It merely reflects the subject, and this mirror is reminding you, instantly, of what you are *not*.

Initially, there is some struggle because nobody asks 'Who am I?' We always ask: "Who are you?" Or "Who is she?" Or "How do I get to know her?" [*Laughter*]

But 'Who am I?' Nobody is asking this question. Why? Perhaps because there cannot be any satisfactory answer to this question. How can the 'I' be found or seen? And by whom will it be discovered?

I started by saying nobody is asking this question. Perhaps you also will come to discover that nobody is asking this question – or any question, ever! Questions, like anything else, simply appear, compelled by some unknowable power!

Beingness brought itself here to be reminded it is not an object. It's not at the mercy of time and space and events. It is the witness of them, the unconcerned and impersonal witness to all and any phenomenon.

It, the Beingness, enjoys being a person, as a role – and that's fine. It does this without losing or altering anything of itself. It exhibits superficial likes and dislikes, but being illusory in nature, their effects are inconsequential, and so they leave no footprints in the consciousness. Realising this, your life and the telling of it becomes a 'writing on water' – you cannot read it a minute later – it's gone!

Beingness does not have to hold onto a history of itself. Mind is like wind. Being is like space. It's the business of the wind to roam about – that is its nature. But space, being infinite, does not roam about. You are like space, formless and unbound. Know this.

That consciousness which is unmoving, effortless, still-beyond-the-concept-of-stillness, does not *know* itself as such. Yet, there is this strange paradox that out of itself arises in manifestation: all this compassion, all this love that it shows for itself in the form of humanity, in the form of 'other' – when searched for, this 'other' cannot really be found.

[*Silence*]

Fear may come as the mental self is moving away from the apparent known into the apparent unknown. The idea we hold of ourselves, which is so prone to feelings of vulnerability, imperfection and timidity, needs constant reassurance; it fears surrendering to the unknown, picturing this as an unfair abandoning of power without guarantee. It senses deep unease and mistrust: "If I let go all of my self-control, then there is no me to take care of my life any more! I might end up being one of these hairy 'babas' you see wandering the streets ... no, no, I don't want that!"

Suddenly that boring office job seems really appealing!

[*Laughter*]

... Can I ask you something about fear, Mooji? Can I tell you that sometimes I feel as if fear is actually poisoning my life? And yet right now, sitting here with you, I'm amazed at how this fear comes!

Why not be amazed at how this fear goes? [*Laughter*]
In the moment of seeing it, it is *not*. How often we are brought to some edge where doom seems

99

inevitable: "Oh my God, I'm going to be swallowed by this monster!" And in the seeing, what is this monster? Who will be eaten? What will die? Be strong and bold. Say: "Ravish me, swallow me up. I am ready!" But don't cover your eyes, be very present and willing to miss nothing in this 'disaster movie'. Watch, from the front seat, your own moment of destruction, if there is one. Will you do this?

Isn't it amazing how quickly that fear goes! Isn't it amazing to see that nothing is actually touching you when you are space-like awareness! Isn't it an incredible discovering that this entire existence is nothing but a Divine play, a great seeming – and that it can be *enjoyed* as a great seeming! That 'I' who will travel to Pondicherry in the morning is also a great seeming. Enjoy the journey!

But Mooji, fear is literally ... all that I've done, actually, has somehow been dictated by fear. It's really hard to 'enjoy the journey' when fear jumps on one, when it really blows out ... Then there's no real peace ... just feeling lost ...

Yes, yes, some fierce throbbing can come, it may come with such force, you might feel completely helpless. There may be some sense of being caught, of being ambushed by old fears or patterns that appear so loud, you are unable to inquire into them in that moment. Then don't inquire; just hand yourself over to the burning, let it just happen. This you must do. Don't fight.

Welcome this moment. Don't embrace it, but *allow* it, and it will become momentous freedom! Become skilled. Become wise through observation. Know the pathways to the ever-free. Remain as the silent awareness and the skill will appear like a good housekeeper who comes and sweeps your house clean. This is Grace serving Grace.

I will fight on!

Oh no! Stop fighting. Enough fighting! Look how tired you have become through this unnecessary struggling. Who and where is the enemy?

It seems everywhere!

This is the drama and the antic of the mind soaked in delusion. Now, try a new approach: hand your existence over to existence itself. Stop swimming. Abandon the urge to save yourself. Do it now. I am here watching. Don't entertain the thought, "No! I can't! I cannot reject effort!" That's what makes it painful, you see. In letting go, letting be, there is the peace, silence and clarity that arise from complete abandonment. Let life be. [*Mooji inhales and exhales deeply*] ... aaaaah ... yes.

[*Another questioner*] *Mooji, who lets go?*

Not an individual. Not any person. It is the mistaken idea that a 'person' can do or undo action to bring about freedom which leads to all confusion, struggle and frustration, you see. It is the Beingness itself which lets go of the sense of being a person. This can be expressed another way: a sense of release or letting go occurs spontaneously within the Self in accordance with its inner wish to be freed from psychological suffering due to mistaken identification with the body and mind functioning. When release from the spell of the illusory ego occurs, instead of the anticipated crisis imagined, mental space, lightness and joy prevail.

So, letting go is not a grand initiation: "Sooooo, today, everybody Let Go!" [*Laughter*] No. It is an inner quality, a subtle intuition. A gentle opening appears and a fresh flowing begins – a flow of Grace.

[*Silence*]

[*Mooji returns to the original questioner*] ... You were going to say something more?

It's just that ... well ... this fear attacks very often. There've been nights when fear comes five or six times. Fears jump out of nowhere, you know ...

Yes, yes ... and where did they go?

Well ... they just left ... in the end, they just left ... thank God! [*Laughter*]

But where did they go? They came out of nowhere, where did they go?

I don't know, Mooji ... sometimes, I've tried to catch hold of them, but, they just ... left! [*Laughter*]

Somehow, out of nowhere, unexpectedly — Grace appears and removes the dirt from your eyes and a thorn from your heart!

But when the fear is there, it's so strong, so suddenly there ... it comes so fast! But when it's gone, it's as if it ... I don't know how to express it ...

I don't invite or encourage anyone to try to make sense of this happening. It is as though some kind of mysterious taxidermy is taking place, by which you are being scooped out from inside and filled up with emptiness. Hand your existence to existence and stay quiet. It is a good thing you don't have to write a polished thesis about this, you don't have that burden. As soon as it comes — it's gone!

[*Laughter*]

But you, you are not gone, you are here to witness the subtlest announcing of anything arising in you. Even if it is this fast [*Mooji snaps his fingers*], you are faster still. Why? Because you are here to witness even lightning speed. You are the quickest by remaining as that effortless stillness!

* * *

... You know, Mooji, I think I don't understand this self-inquiry thing at all. I don't know ... I don't get it ... I really have to be totally honest.

Yes, yes, total honesty is what is required. [*Laughter*]

[*Another questioner*] *Sorry, I have exactly the same question. I don't understand either. Am I supposed to locate 'me'? I've been attempting this for years ...*

[*First questioner*] *Yes, me too ...*

[*Second questioner*] *... and I don't really know what I am supposed to be doing ...*

[First *questioner*] *Me neither!* [*Huge laughter*]

What comedy! 'What to do?' is the mantra of the mind. Silence is the response but the mind misses this excellent counsel. 'What to do, what to do, what to do?' – who employed you to do anything in the first place? [*Laughter*]
 Okay. Start again. Work with me! Forget about all you've already heard. Start from scratch. Words are pouring out – "I cannot understand, I, I, I, am I supposed to look here or there? It's too much for *me*!" Who speaks these words? I wish to be introduced to that one. [*Laughter*]
 You! [*Mooji points to one questioner*] Respond!

[*Questioner sighs*] *But I can't ... I don't understand the inquiry. My mind becomes confused and agitated.*

Don't understand inquiry. Don't think, look! Who is it that is saying: "*I can't, I* don't understand … " Does it have a shape, size or body?

How am I supposed to look for it when I don't …

'I' is what, again? [*Laughter*] 'I' is what? *Who* is baffled?

Me! [*Laughter*] *I am absolutely bamboozled! I don't have a clue!*

Yes, yes. You are aware of bamboozled-ness. And if you are not bamboozled, then you say, "Aaaah, I am delighted!" So, the bamboozled state and the delighted one, you'll be aware of both. Therefore you must be apart. Be there … where you already are. That place which you cannot divide.

Can I say something? Am I supposed to ask: "Who am I that is aware of being bamboozled?" Is that how it works? [Laughter] No, seriously ….

Seriously? Off with your head!!! [*Mooji slices his hand through the air, mimicking the movement of a sword*]

[*Laughter. Then … Silence*]

* * *

[*Another questioner*] *Aaaaaah, this 'I' has gone! I'm trying to locate where it's gone …*

It's gone, now, but which 'I' is trying to locate it? Don't think, look! Behold, the absurdness of the mind all venerate!

I'm trying to feel it by going into the heart, I think ... well, somewhere in my centre or ... no, it's not quite that either ... it's more that I ...

Shut up!!

[*Silence*]

* * *

... When I am inquiring at home I just say: "Who is feeling this emotion?" And then the next question is: "What is behind this?"

Okay, that's it! You are fired! [*Huge laughter*]

And can I inquire into who is fired? [*More laughter*]

Just for now, you are fired! Your mind is fired. But it's going to keep on showing up for work ... [*Laughter*]
   Just keep quiet like this. Just be quiet. You have nothing to 'do,' nothing to 'get'. Don't touch the idea you are missing something. Don't touch any idea at all! Okay? I will take care of you. You are no more your business. You are my business. Okay?

Yes ... okay ...

[Small laughter ... then long silence]

... Thank you, Mooji.

[Silence]

You seem to believe in a God.
What is God for you,
and where is He?

I don't 'believe' in God –
I know God intimately.

God is the core of my being,
and all beings, without exception.

God is the originator of all forms, being formless.

God is infinite, and therefore pervades all that exists.

God is beyond all.

God is pure consciousness,
unknowable by the mind,
shining within all,
as the sense

'I am'.

Could you say you are God?

What is your view on the various religions of the world?

All is good, even the irreligious is good. All play their part and serve their purpose; yet I stand apart, detached from them all. Good or bad, I have no need of them. This is not a position of judgement or arrogance. It simply means that all that arises within the scope of my perceptive field – such as thinking, seeing, feeling, being – necessarily must depend upon my being here present to see and know of its appearance. Without 'I' – nothing is.

I, the necessary conscious presence, is the crucial, the most important factor, throughout. Without me, nothing exists – for if I do not exist, then there cannot be anything else apart from myself to know of the existence or non-existence of any phenomena.

So, could you say you are God?

I could say I am God, but it would not mean anything, as words cannot contain the speaker of them.

I also cannot be the speaker, for, having thoroughly searched for him, he has never been found in any shape, size or form. God also must exist as a conceptual entity in my mind for me to have knowledge of him, however subtle. He cannot exist outside of my own consciousness, therefore He must, at best, be the consciousness I am.

Purely speaking, whatever it is that functions as the searcher, I am also not that, since I witness the sense of searching happening without any tangible seeker.

All that may be said is that what I am must be more subtle and earlier than even the sense 'I am,' the intuitive sense of subjective existence, for the 'I am' is also perceived. Therefore what I truly am, what *is*, must be the subtlest principle. This principle must be the only constant, for all 'other' is what comes and goes and is witnessed inside the unchanging.

Do you believe in a personal God? Like Hindus believe in Ishwara, Muslims in Allah, Christians in Christ?

For me, God is both personal and impersonal, is and is not, and beyond any of those ideas. He is there, naturally, when the mood inside me yearns for him as God. Then I enjoy Him as father, friend, presence, grace, mystical knowledge, benevolence and compassionate love. Otherwise, he is not: meaning he is merged in my consciousness as pure, quality-less Being, beyond belief, beyond duality.

I don't encourage any theological or philosophical debate about God, for these are mostly a distraction and a waste of energy. They don't bring about any real insight or significant shift away from dry intellectualism. Avoid this!

This is what mostly drew me to you: this balance of Jnana and Bhakti [knowledge and devotion]. *This is what I find unique in your expression. It is this warmth which makes what you say come alive for me, for it opens the path of trust towards your teaching, which is most important in my view. I want to thank you for this.*

[*Silence*]

*When the various rivers flow
into the great Ocean,
they lose their individual names
and become Ocean only.*

*While the raindrop is falling
towards the Ocean,
the fear of discontinuation
may seem greater than
the anticipated joy
of merging with the Infinite.*

*But when it touches Ocean,
can it tell the traveller's tale?*

Can it speak of this meeting?

Emptiness walking
in the form of a human being

Be empty. Be emptiness, this is the secret. Try it. Read a book but stay completely empty – reading happens in perfect clarity, the words remain on the page. Enjoy a conversation, also in complete emptiness – conversation happens in natural flow. Observe, and gradually you will come to see that all existence is occurring in empty awareness. Like this, you realise that perception, activity, dreaming, everything, happens as natural expression of the Beingness in manifestation. In fact, life functions with greater clarity, harmony and spontaneity without the assumed management and subjectivity of the 'I'-thought – a revolutionary discovery!

Look for your beginning and your end. Hmmm ... [*Mooji closes his eyes*] ... mere notions.

Who are you? Emptiness walking in the form of a human being. Forget yourself and discover your Self. Let what you know mentally be confirmed with your entire being. This is the purpose of your coming to satsang: to discover what you have imagined you have lost. Your presence, body and mind will ooze that realisation with such power and beauty that other beings, thirsting for truth, will come to take shelter and shade in the peace of your presence.

Everywhere you go, people carry their 'rucksacks' of personality. Even on the beach everybody has one! [*Laughter*] What is this rucksack? It is ego-identity. "I am unique. I care for myself, body and mind. See how it has paid off – observe my beauty!" [*More laughter*] They can't let go of this bag of dust. All the while, it is simply nature that is playing through each form in unique ways. It expresses judgements and preferences superficially. It acts as though it is an autonomous individual unconnected with other sentient beings. In fact, the opposite is true.

Take the example of the wave and the ocean. The movement of each wave has the total ocean underneath and behind it. No wave, including a tsunami, has autonomy. It cannot say, "I will go this way by myself, I will not follow the others." When there is strong identification with the instrument through which the life-force and consciousness experiences, that identity seems to take the qualities of the instrument as itself and become smothered with arrogance and pride. Perhaps it even feels, secretly, "The world would be a better place if everyone was like me."

I say, be a spectator not a dictator. Learn to observe this ego-sense through constant discernment of what is real from what is not. The unreal is changeful. It manifests as mind, mood, time and relationships. The real is the invisible within the visible. It is the single seer which itself cannot be seen phenomenally. It is known only by negating all that is knowable, quantifiable, relative and variable. As one recognises and identifies as the impersonal witnessing, the unfolding stream of thoughts, effects and events are observed to shine in their momentary 'here-and-gone-ness', but leave no footprint in the consciousness.

As ultimate understanding ripens, it dissolves the personal idea of self. Things are not happening to a 'me' anymore, they merely happen of their own accord – but there is no chaos here. Instead, a real harmony is felt and witnessed, held within boundless joy and still- ness. Everything we do, everything we perceive, arises from and in emptiness. This emptiness is not stagnant, not sterile, not a blank. It is quality-less, like space. All this magnificent universe is dancing in unborn aware- ness. All is sourced in That.

That's a beautiful way to describe it, Mooji, 'the magnificent uni- verse dancing in unborn awareness' – such beautiful words ...

No-one is able to convey it through words alone. I don't think even the pure-tongued Buddha did it. Neither Papaji nor Sri Ramana Maharshi could do it. I don't think anyone throughout history, however inspired, has done it. However, their presence somehow, having merged in the source, the single Truth ... [*Long silence ... there are tears in Mooji's eyes ...*] ... shone brightly with the light and peace of that pure Awareness Self. This is undeniable.

115

I lack any spiritual training. Perhaps this is why, though I love hearing you speak, I find it a little difficult to really grasp what I have heard ...

All that is required you already possess in abundance. Be sure of this. Some people come to satsang, they speak no English ... and still, something resonates deep within them and their minds fall effortlessly into silent recognition of the origin. It is beyond language and intellect. Even animals have come.

Indeed, satsang is not only for human beings. Satsang is for all beings. The word 'satsang' means 'association with Truth'. All beings, graced with the urge to simply *be*, respond to Truth.

Don't fill your mind with instructions

Place your hand on your heart and then say something from there.

I feel a strong urge to surrender. I see how my desires for passing pleasures and security do not serve me. I think I'm at a crisis point. I see something in you that inspires great confidence in me but I feel I have far to go yet.

How many metres or kilometres? Sitting right here, where do you need to go to be more here than you are right now? Give up these kinds of thoughts and strivings. See if you lose anything of real worth in doing so.

I've spent so much of my life on a path, trying to get somewhere, trying to find something!

This is your blessing in disguise! It enabled you to seek out truth unrelentingly. It brought you here. Initially it cannot be avoided, this roaming about on 'the path.' Through trust and faith, deeper and deeper discoveries will unfold. They will bring joy and, of course, joy is naturally known to the beingness! There is no difference between the joy of sexual union, the joy of a politician winning the local election, or the joy that arises in meditation. But the joy arising from

117

knowledge of the Self is impersonal, fresh, unassociated and timeless. Once this recognition has happened through real understanding, there is a beautiful loosening, there remains no mental rigidity. Everything is seen, lived and experienced as the play of consciousness.

I still have a question, though. How does that recognition happen? How does that shift in perspective occur?

Do not fill your mind with instructions. They suffocate your spontaneity! Throughout your life, you have piled up instruction after instruction, one on to top another. Have you been able to carry them out?

So what should I do? I believe everything you've said today, I trust your words completely. But I don't know what to do now ...

What need you do? What can you do? Keep quiet or dive inward in the direction I keep pointing to, that sign-less core. Belief is good, and trust is better; but direct knowledge and experience are the highest.

As a result of this seeing, what remains is that unbroken experience called reality.

Freedom from being someone

When the sought is found,
the seeker disappears.

I spent thirty-five years in a school of Advaita Yoga, and after
all those years, one day I just walked out. I realised everything
I'd learned was directed at the mind, and that what is true is
so present that it cannot be found in the mind. But still, there
is an idea that, in order to be free, I should experience myself as
'everywhere-ness'. And yet the sticking-point is that experience
remains in the mind and body.

You should forget about trying to experience yourself as everywhere-ness. Any attitude of setting a goal
is misleading. If an experience comes like that, then
fine! It will be momentary. Such a phenomenon may
occur spontaneously as a flash or spark from Grace, or
may arise from your practices, yoga, mantras or prayers.
Everything is experienced in and by consciousness. It
is the all-possible, the unlimited. As long as a body is
present, and the vital force is there, the sense 'I am'
along with other thought-activity and phenomena will
be there also.

Duality entraps me. I lose focus and end up in a forest of
conflict and confusion.

It need not be so. Consider: can you experience anything if the concept of separation or division is not there? Could you even taste knowledge of yourself without duality? There is no need to escape from or erase duality, for without duality there cannot be experience. Therefore, duality is not a mistake but the vital tool of creation.

Enjoy the all-encompassing movie called life with all its tears and laughter, dreams, desires and loathing, all its devotion, pranks and prayers. The full spectrum of consciousness in expression is available and beautiful when seen through eyes emptied through understanding and grace.

There is no particular 'way' to be. Relax, be yourself and remain open and quiet in the face of all that life manifests. Just remember: you are the seen, the seer and beyond both, as the unborn Awareness. It could also be said you are the person, the knower of the person and the space in which both appear.

So what is the work then? Just to rest in emptiness?

Yes, what else? Or better still, rest in emptiness *as* emptiness. In fact, that 'work' or 'practice,' if you want to call it that, will become increasingly spontaneous, without any sense that there is someone carrying it out. It will arise by itself and take care of all your affairs. So the sense of being a person, of having particular personality and preferences, need not be felt as injurious at all when understanding is there. It is just the functioning of manifestation in the role of a person. This play arises in consciousness, and it is being witnessed from nowhere. Or, if you prefer, from everywhere – same thing. Don't stick any label on it.

I can see now what my error was, I kind of wanted to experience myself as That, but it is not possible!

Exactly! 'That' is so one with itself that it is incapable of seeing itself. Take the example of a knife which can cut through so many objects but cannot cut itself, being one inseparable unit. Or, similarly, a scale which weighs many objects but cannot weigh itself. What Is cannot perceive itself, being already one with itself.

So, the freedom of which you have spoken is the freedom from being someone?

Yes. Ultimately, it is freedom from even the concept of freedom. It is the end of striving. We put all our attention, all our efforts and energy, into becoming the best someone we can be. That is natural, that is the whole story of mankind. But it is not freedom.

By all means live the highest expression you can. Change what you feel does not serve your truth, follow your heart's promptings, but do not take the expression to be a definition of the Self. Enjoy, with gratitude, your life – as a gift from Life, as an expression of God, as the dance of the cosmos – while

121

remaining throughout as the formless seer. The sage looks into a mirror at the pictures appearing as himself, but he is not confused.

He remains as unalterable Being in the shrine of emptiness.

Consciousness plays
as everything

There seems to be the idea that something is missing.

Consciousness in its human expression is always hungry
for something. As soon as it touches the sense of autonomy, of individuality, there manifests almost spontaneously a feeling that something is lacking, so it is always
trying to find something – a sense of completeness, a
sense of stability, of coming home. It may be felt in
different ways, like a need for healing, a need for re-
pairing, or for progress, or for all of these things. This
tendency seems deeply-rooted in the human psyche.
'Something is missing,' it is thought. 'If it wasn't, surely I wouldn't feel like this! Surely Jesus didn't feel like
this. I feel miserable so, obviously, I cannot be what he
is, for he is pure.' This is an assumption. Who said that
in the morning, Jesus didn't wake up feeling a little
grumpy? [*Laughter*] Who said that when he was walking with disciples that he didn't feel irritated by their
petty squabbles? Who can say? That time in the mar-
ketplace when he saw people gambling in the temple,
he snapped: "This place is not for gambling, get out!" I
am sure he didn't say: "Pleeease, don't be offended but
… " [*Laughter*] Who says he was without such feelings?
Who said he is so different from you?

He was God and Man. Do you know what this means? It means he was aware of himself as ego-less being, moved by God-force and Grace. This too you are. Why is your mind always wriggling to escape the obvious? Why, when you are directed to this clear truth, do you prevaricate? When the mind-set feels challenged by the looking, it goes into avoidance! 'Better we practise a bit more! Let's go step-by-step, gently, gently ... ' [*Laughter*] Something seems to be avoiding being exposed. What is it? Look at that.

Now, understand that this way of avoiding, it also is the play of consciousness. Consciousness plays the sage, the seeker, and the fool. What else can it be? Mind is the expression of consciousness. Sometimes consciousness manifests as tremendous stupidity. Who else can do it? Recognising this, one becomes at ease with all things.

I saw a man on television – this is a true story! – who said he had fallen in love with a cow. He said this in front of the whole nation. [*Laughter*] "I am deeply in love with her! And she is in love with me! Look in her eyes!" he said, pointing to the cow – who, it must be said, had a look of utter boredom on its face! [*Laughter*] And he could not understand why people didn't bless their relationship [*More laughter*], or why they should think it wrong that he should wish to marry this cow! [*Laughter*] And he was totally serious. He had children also, they went to school, everybody teased them, saying, "Your father loves a cow!" [*Laughter*] He said people didn't understand. In his mind he was clear about this affair. He was completely at peace with himself.

What else but consciousness is performing this play?

Consciousness plays as everything, as each and every role in the entire play of Creation.

There are some people who come to this deep awareness in a short space of time. In the course of a single meeting with Truth, their minds are resolved into complete silence.

I had such a realisation a few days ago, Mooji, but the mind came back — and with greater force than before! Why was that?

Take this example: if you shoot a rabbit with a tranquiliser gun, he drops right away. Some people are like that. In the hearing of truth, the heart opens and mind falls irretrievably into silence, no further words will come. But for others, it's more like if you shoot a rhino – off it goes! Buggudupp, buggudupp, buggudupp! [*Laughter*] But you don't need to chase him. You can just keep walking in his direction. Because even though he may carry on running a little further, he is gradually slowing down as the effect of the tranquilliser takes over. Eventually, he too will drop. Somewhere you will find him fallen, heavy as a tree, happily snoring. [*Laughter*] Then you can touch him – "Mr. Rhino, how are you? Why do you run so?" Some egos are like that. At the first blast, the hit of the truth, instantly mind rebels – buggudupp, buggudupp, buggudupp! And they're off! [*Laughter*]

There is no fault with that. This also is the expression and play of consciousness. What to do?

Consciousness pervades all that manifests. Even the Elements are consciousness. And the perceiving of them is consciousness. The perceiving of the perceiving happens in the unspeakable, the unnameable. And you are That.

Consciousness manifests as diversity, and the perceiving of this diversity – of changefulness, of blessedness, of cursedness, of healing, of pain and joy, of bondage and freedom – takes place while all the while undergoing no change in itself. It is just like when one dreams. In our dreams, we see a world full of diversity, fashioned just like this world. Emotions, thought, creativity – all is there in that dream state. One meets people speaking languages one is unable to understand in this world. One would have to undergo language-study here in order to communicate with them. When one awakens, one finds all this occurred in one's mind only.

The same is true of the Real waking state.

How can it be that that which remains eternally unchanging manifests as the changeful? And seems to undergo some kind of hypnosis of believing itself to be separated from itself? And then strives towards knowing itself through the mind? How can it be that it creates

all this dreaming, and then also manifests the capacity
to awaken itself from its own self-induced slumber? –
only to realise it has never been asleep! What a strange
thing! [*Laughter*] Such paradoxes! Everything explodes
into paradoxes! And that which witnesses them? It is
beyond paradoxes.

Leave it alone. You are that within which even the
advice 'Leave it alone' is heard as nothing more than
a soft ephemeral whisper inside itself. Who is there to
carry out any advice?

Each one, in your own unique flow, has been brought
to this moment, to this point. How much further to go?
Towards what? For what purpose? From monkey mind,
to monk's mind, to no mind – and still no change in
you. No change. Something knows this intuitively. You
are untouched.

[*Silence*]

Keep your mind inside your heart.

Could that not be called a practice?

If you want to call it a practice, fine. Why not? Nothing wrong with the word or act of 'practice' at all. Sri
Nisargadatta Maharaj was a perfect *jnani*, and still,
every day, three or four times a day, he sang *bhajans*
with great vigour. Did he feel, "Oh no, I mustn't do this
any longer. I am a sage now. What will people think?!"
No. His being was in perfect affinity with everything,

one with the flow of existence. Therefore, his actions were spontaneous, uninhibited. Don't suppress your dance in order to play some role. Be yourself.

It is said that he who seeks God, finds himself. And that he who seeks himself, finds God. Whether your path is the path of devotion, surrender or wisdom, the end is one.

It is just this.

Your words have a finality about them. I think I'm just waiting for the final chop.

Who will notice this chop? Who will know 'I have received the last chop?' Leave aside the idea of a final chop, and also this waiting for something to happen.

The axe is falling but the head is still talking! Now the axe has fallen, still the head is talking!

[*Silence*]

You are This.

Thank you.

Don't carry anything with you

Anything that you can describe, all your ideas, leave them aside just for now. Anything you can expect, remember, or imagine, leave aside. Stay as what remains.

'I' is the generator and support for all other thoughts. The magnetism of some thoughts will feel stronger than others. Those thoughts will strongly reinforce the sense of 'I', in fact they arise together, forcefully. In that moment, the clarity of the original Self may seem to be masked by the intensity of the identification with 'I' and whatever sensation it has hooked onto. See for yourself: at this very moment, try to catch hold of this 'I', using its current fascination as a scent. Sniff out the 'I'. See if it is anything at all.

[*Silence*]

Truly, what you are searching for is where you are searching from.

Don't touch the idea that something, some action, stops you from being what you are. Examined, it is found to be untrue. Nothing stops you except the idea that something stops you. Hold onto this idea and it will suck your strength away.

One must really want this ...

I have three options to offer you. One, throw away the idea of a one who wants. Two, ignore all attempts or invitations to reach somewhere or to gain something. Three, if the desire to realise who you really are arises in you, accept it as already the activity of Grace.

It's a kind of suicidal desire as well ...

This suicide is okay. The ego that commits suicide becomes the Self. This suicide is not harmful. This is good suicide. [*Laughter*]

Not much more to hold onto! All the ideas on which I thought I was built, they don't stand up anymore!

Yes, how fortunate! The mind works perfectly without clinging to identity. This is pure mind.

This feels like quite a challenge ...

For whom? Find the one who feels and fears the challenge.

There are a lot of ideas about attachments and ...

'Attachments' are also ideas. I have no teaching to offer. Satsang is not a place for mere learning. For discovering, yes. For deconstruction of all mental and psychological strategies, yes. For a kind of 'ghost-busting', yes. It's a place for dying to the untrue. And, indeed, for ego-suicidal ideas ...

[*Laughter*]

It does feel quite frightening, Mooji ...

Be bold! At the most auspicious opportunity, at the highest possibility for total seeing and clarity to appear, resistance often arises and takes centre stage. What is it that is trying to escape? At the crucial point, be aware of all kinds of excuses and avoidances.

There was once a man who came to my house, and the deeper his inquiry drew him, the more he sought distraction. "Can I go use the bathroom?" he'd ask. "Can I have a glass of water? It's a bit hot in here, can we open the door?" And this was in the middle of winter! [*Laughter*] Finally, I challenged his prevarications. "Can you see what is going on? You are not a prisoner here, you can go anytime you want. Go now if you don't want to be here!" Only then, when exposed, did he manage to steady himself in the inquiry and merge his mind in peace.

* * *

So there is nothing to be done?

Allow yourself to be undone! Let Grace undress you.

Everything that you have done, every practice that you've made, has brought you to this point, right now. There is nothing to regret. Now, keep quiet. Rest yourself, here and now, in the very source of your awareness. In its silence. In its fullness. In its emptiness.

In the absence of that 'I-ego' you imagined you were, there now shines pure presence. And this presence is all-pervading. When ultimate seeing occurs, pure energy is discharged which blesses and energises every other aspect of your expression. Nothing remains to be understood. Projections, opinions, interpretations and ideas drop away and all that is dances its dance in complete freedom.

My Master used to say, "Self reveals itself in a pure mind."

Leave all your intentions aside. Come here naked.

Trust the grace
that brought you here

Understand and trust that Grace is already operating in you. Your being here is impelled by grace. The speaking and the listening leave and enter through the one source. When words and actions arise from the depth of truth, they carry a force, an authority that is capable of imbuing silence and recognition in the listener. It flows with a different frequency, a frequency of total clarity.

Mooji, it seems that your presence and words help to strengthen my resolve to step into — and stay in! — the fire that burns the personal mind.

I don't promise you anything. At best, something said and heard feels provocative, slaps your attention into alertness or focuses it on the unmoving Self. Again, the impulse to step into the fire of self-sacrifice, to lie down on the burning ghat for the ego, this is an impulse arising from Grace itself.

Why does beingness or God bring about such suffering sometimes? Is it that we deserve it?

It is not like that. Suffering enables us to feel compassion and empathy for other beings. It deepens our own being by washing off the slime of the trivial and prepares the soil of the psyche for higher understanding. Adopt an attitude of gratitude in all expressions of life.

It is hard to find one's true purpose. It seems impossible to know what is the correct path and action to take in any given situation.

Why bother with all that? Forget yourself and be happy. Life is not merely a personal journey. It is not only the experiencing of material existence through imagination, emotion and intellect. And there are no reliable how-to-do manuals for how to negotiate life that I am aware of. Only when the sense of the personal, limited 'I' merges with the universal being does the real life begin, and not before. When the ego-identity is isolated and sieved out, pure power is recognised to be already present in you as the witness. Then appropriate responses are simply taking place without any private operator moving them. Only in pure listening, when the listening is not invaded or intruded upon by a personal mind which constantly judges, interprets and clings to the past, does enlightened response take place spontaneously.

I really want to pay attention to the things you're saying, Mooji, but honestly, my mind is just going blank!

In this type of intense probing, it is not unusual for your mind to go blank. Still, you are not the mind. You are that which watches this sense of contraction, or the 'blank' as you put it, and the drifting attention. At this point, the attention easily swings towards trivial things as the ego struggles to keep out of the view of the deeper witness. Stay as one with that which witnesses all appearances, and don't be gullible or quick to purchase the suggestions and judgements pushed up by the mind in its effort to avoid detection.

Truth is that in which even the seeker and the seeking are scrutinised and found to be nothing more than mind's play.

Your questions are not real.
My answers are not real.

World is not real.

Wars and peace are equally unreal.
Aspirations are unreal.
Solutions, unreal.
Nature, unreal.

I, also, am unreal.
You are unreal.

Life itself is unreal.
Death, too, is unreal.

All is illusion. Unreal.

The Self, beyond quality,
time-less, and space-less,
alone is real.

Do you understand?

I do.

You, who understand, are also unreal.

That in which the response "I do" arises and is perceived –
That, alone,

is real.

For the one who knows,
nothing happens

Is discovering our true nature dependent on destiny or is our own effort necessary?

Don't pick up and run off with this idea of destiny. It is enough to say that if effort feels natural then it was destined to arise as such. Whatever the body-mind must go through cannot be avoided. There is great wisdom, order and harmony operating through and as the cosmic play. The point is to grasp the ultimate and timeless message that you are the formless witness only, the unchanging reality behind the moving mind. You appear as a separate entity with volitional powers on account of *Maya*, the cosmic illusion. *Maya* is the power which enables the Beingness to taste and enjoy the flavour of itself as existence. Within that, it undergoes some apparent maturing, which is not a quality of the Absolute, but is most important because consciousness cannot really know itself when it lacks the ripeness of subtle understanding and direct experience.

These days many people have heard and read *Advaita* philosophy or *Zen* teachings, but the truth they point to often stays only in the mind and intellect. They don't dissolve their identities. Instead, they keep on collecting more and more knowledge. They often make comments like: "No one exists, and meditation is useless, for who is there to meditate? Belief in a God is superstition or a sign of mental and emotional weakness. All those rituals, what's the use?" And so on. Such cynicism is just arrogance. It shows that they are far from being like the Buddha they imagine themselves to be. If truth is not one's direct experience, then life itself will sooner or later expose any hypocrisy. Burn the ego in the fire of devotion until all pride is washed away.

The awakened mind respects all ways of Being, all forms of devotion, all religions, even the fanatical, without judgement or dismissal, knowing all emanate as expressions from the one single source. That's what is so lovable in Ramakrishna and all the saints and sages: they each displayed this broadness of outlook and compassionate being. They were free from feelings of special-ness and pride. With skill and compassion, their teaching adapted itself spontaneously to suit the maturity of those who came to them. To some they advised prayer or meditation if that was in affinity with their mental state, or until they became mature enough to inquire directly into their nature.

There is no contradiction between the path of love and the path of wisdom. The sense of maturing lasts the duration of each apparent lifetime, and happens against the unchanging background of the Absolute. For the one who knows, nothing happens. Yet even after 'awakening', there continues to be the sense of deepening and evolving and there is a sweetness and beauty in that. Don't make the mistake of thinking you have transcended God or that you have annihilated duality. If there is still a *you* to claim such things, right there, ignorance prevails.

Simply, keep quiet. The delivered mind is one with the law of causation.

In recognition of
the stillness, joy and love

which are the fragrance
of your own pure heart,

Keep Quiet …

Parting words

Beloved, be still and know the magnificence of the intuition – 'I am'. I am one with you as witness and conscious presence, timelessly unchanging. Recognise your own real self and be happy. We are not our thoughts, emotions, memories or conditioning, but formless Being, eternally changing, yet – unchanging. Be integrated with that silent space behind the moving mind. Be one with That – that within which this grand dance of manifestation is perceived. Knowing this, the mind is stilled.

Be willing to lay down, to leave aside, the itch to tell stories, to share opinions and projections born of delusion – the outcome of false identification. Observe the unbroken silence from which all springs. Recognise yourself as attribute-less Being, as beyond the changeful, and be happy.

Be still and know 'I am'. Rest in 'I Am' – as I Am.

We are the unbroken and unbreakable presence behind all phenomena. Do not any longer indulge the fickle tendencies of the ego-mind to stray towards meaningless dribbles. They may seem harmless enough at the time but they gradually stupefy the mind and lead to a build-up of inner chatter and restlessness which then appear to tyrannise the peaceful Beingness.

Again, be reminded: be disciplined, vigilant and strict with yourself by resisting the pull to go with the mind-flow, so that gradually the mind and attention become habituated to remaining in the heart-core. This is true *sadhana*, your true work. This alone leads to unbroken silence and stillness of mind – the true goal and purpose of conscious and intelligent existence. It is noble living beyond the concept of noble living, and it is true self-honouring.

When Consciousness identifies with body-mind, the result is egoism – which is the root and cause of all suffering. Be determined to slay this dragon. He is slain through prayer, surrender and devotion, and he is slain with the sword of self-inquiry. The illusory 'I' cannot prevail under the scrutiny and force of self-investigation. Do not indulge any sentiment towards the ego. Cease identifying and supporting what is effectively suffocating your peace.

Make your stand with Truth.

Hold the attention in the heart. Persevere through any discomfort or resistance that arises in much the same way as you may have had to do when you first began your inquiry. Like this, the ego sense, which thrives on the oxygen of your attention, interest and belief, is gradually extinguished.

Trust my words when I say you are already free; act on them as though you already knew them to be true. Let your life be a living satsang, a steady attitude and application of self-inquiry and surrender to truth. Lose or shun the stubbornness, pride, resistance and cynicism that slow you down. Recognising the false, you need not search for the real, for the false is seen from the ground of the real. Be humble; humility is wisdom. It is wise to seek help until you go beyond the need for help. The seed of expanding insight and deepening understanding which leads to complete peace is already germinating in your heart.

Trust this.

Awareness is not on the other side of working through any process, for awareness is already that through which any striving is recognised. How true is the old saying 'What you are looking for is already where you are looking from.'

You are truth.

You are That in which the universe manifests.

Self-inquiry is the mirror in which the timeless is recognised and timelessly reflected.

You are That!

Surrendering oneself to the inner Guru, the Lord of all, is another way into the recognising of this in the heart.

We are ever one as truth and love.

We are the unicity of Being in its dance as existence.

Self romancing Self is the dance called satsang.

Satsang is unending. Knowing this is allowing yourself to be danced by God.

It is my good fortune and privilege to announce and thus share with you this sweet message from within.

My joy is to watch this play of awakening to the divine and eternal within ourselves. Just as we say the sun rises and sets though the sun never moves – it is the earth which turns away from the sun – even so, the real Self never moves or leaves, being infinite and infinitely present. It is the earth-mind which turns away from the sun-heart.

Therefore, keep your attention in that which is prior to attention, in which both attention and inattention are perceived, and which is beyond both.

I have no interest in giving you any theoretical knowledge, however sublime, nor to create in you beautiful experiences or satsang nostalgia. It is enough if you awaken with clarity and conviction to the unchanging truth you already are.

Stay here!
Here is all there is.
Be Happy.

In loving Oneness,

For information about Mooji's work and schedule,
you are welcome to visit the website

www.mooji.org

Acknowledgements

So much gratitude ...

... to all the friends in Ireland, England, Italy, America, and India, who supported, participated in, recorded, transcribed and selected the satsangs from which these dialogues have been drawn.

... to all those who were involved in the editing, proofreading, formatting, design, printing and publishing – Martha Callejas, Antonio Congedo, Karam Roberto De Rinaldis, Martine Fordham, Shanti Frie, Brian Jackson, Francois Jonquet, Lee Hogan Kerrigan, Clelia Marinelli, Ian McNicholl, Suzanne Montenegro, Gayatri (Nageena), Mohan Nair, Girija Nair, Monica Onore, Baba Om, Paola Paldo, Thyago Ryan, Hannah Santos Lã and Zenji.

... to all, for all,
Om Shanti.

About Mooji

Anthony Paul Moo-Young, affectionately known as 'Mooji', was born on 29 January 1954 in Port Antonio, Jamaica. In 1969, he moved to the UK and he is presently living in Brixton, London.

In 1987, a chance meeting with a Christian mystic was to be a life-changing encounter for Mooji. It brought him, through prayer, into the direct experience of the Divine within. As his spiritual consciousness awakened, a deep inner transformation began which unfolded in the form of many miraculous experiences and mystical insights. A great peace entered his being, and has remained ever since.

In 1993, Mooji felt compelled to visit India. Whilst there, an inexplicable pull drew him into the presence of Sri Harilal Poonja, the renowned Advaita Master, also known as 'Papaji'. "If you wish to realise the Truth," Papaji told him, "*you* must completely disappear." Through the power and grace of his Master's presence, his mind irreversibly merged with its source.

Since 1999, Mooji has been sharing this realisation in the form of spontaneous encounters, retreats, satsang intensives, skype dialogues and one-to-one meetings with the many seekers who visit him, from all parts of the world, in search of the direct experience of truth.

Presently Mooji shares satsang in the UK, Italy, India, Brazil, America, Germany and Spain. He is ever open to meeting sincere seekers of Truth, whatever their background.

ༀ

Attempting to identify with the Source
is an idea arising in the Source.

You are already That.

The Little Lost Wave

Once upon a time, there was a little wave who'd grown tired and restless, worn out from all her to-ing and fro-ing between horizon and shore. One day, she heard of a Great Ocean where there were no restless wanderings at the mercy of the tides, where everything was quiet and full of love. A huge desire arose in her to find this peaceful place, but — she didn't know where to begin.

"Do you know the way to the Great Ocean?" she asked the other waves as they passed. One wave, an Elder who was greatly weighed down with seaweed, told her, "I've heard of this Ocean, but it is very far away and would take many lifetimes to reach." Another wave gurgled, "I've heard that if we are very kind and gentle waves, and live very, very good lives, then when we die, the Great Ocean is where we will find ourselves." "You're all deluded, there is no such thing as this Ocean," added a swirling wave, cynically.

"Hey! Come with me!" called a fresh wave with a friendly voice. "I know a wise wave who has actually been to the Great Ocean and knows it well. I will introduce you to him!" And off they went.

As they were leaving, another wave grumbled, "Crazy kids! Why all this waste of energy searching for some mythical place? Why not be content with what you have?"

Soon, they arrived at the abode of the wise wave.

"Please, wise wave, can you show me the Great Ocean?" begged the little wave.

The wise wave started laughing, in deep, warm gusts that sent spray skipping across the surface of the water. "What do you imagine the Great Ocean is, my child?"

"I've heard it is a wonderful place, full of beauty and joy, that there is love and lasting peace there," trembled the little wave.

The wise wave laughed some more. "You are searching for this Great Ocean, little friend, but you are Ocean itself! How funny that you are not aware of this!"

This made the little wave more confused and a bit annoyed. "How can that be? I don't see any ocean. All I see are waves, waves and more waves!"

"That's because you think you are a wave," the wise wave smiled.

At this, the little wave splashed against a nearby rock in frustration. "I don't understand anything you are saying! Can you show me the Great Ocean, yes or no?" she pressed impatiently.

"Okay, okay, determined little friend," said the wise wave, "but -- before I do, would you mind diving below and massaging my aching feet?"